FINDING YOUR FEET IN BERLIN

GIULIA PINES

FINDING YOUR FEET IN BERLIN

A Guide to Making a Home in the Hauptstadt

With photographs by Paul Sullivan

BERLIN STORY VERLAG

IMPRINT

Pines, Giulia:
Finding Your Feet in Berlin
1st edition—Berlin: Berlin Story Verlag 2014
ISBN: 978-3-95723-000-3

© Berlin Story Verlag GmbH
Unter den Linden 40, 10117 Berlin
Tel.: (030) 20 91 17 80
Fax: (030) 20 45 38 41
E-Mail: Service@BerlinStory-Verlag.de
Cover design: Norman Bösch (cover picture © Pedelecs by Wikivoyage and
Wikicommons | CC-BY-SA 3.0 | http://creativecommons.org/licenses/by-sa/3.0/
deed.en; author photo © Harald Franzen)
Composition: Nadin Wildt
Photography: Paul Sullivan

WWW.BERLINSTORY-VERLAG.DE

CONTENT

AN INTRODUCTION

Most people don't happen upon it by chance. They read an article, hear a snippet of a travel story from a friend, or feel that unmistakable pull towards a place where history is celebrated, all-encompassing, engulfing—not just a side note. In an era where everything and everyone is connected and nothing remains undiscovered for long, Berlin can offer a respite: a place still in the midst of its own discovery, doing just fine at a more laid-back pace quite contradictory to the rest of the world, and even to the rest of Germany.

I wasn't one of those people. I felt a pull of a different sort, attracted by the one thing most new arrivals seem to avoid almost by instinct: the German language. A university graduate back in 2008, a New Yorker who had never really left New York, I had only the vague sense that I wanted to experience something different, along with a cursory interest in learning German. A friend told me about the Goethe-Institut, and with that, it was decided: I would go to learn a new language, attempting the study abroad year I'd never had. And if it was going to be Germany, it would have to be Berlin. It was only after I had booked my plane ticket and registered for my first German class that I began to hear murmurings of what I was in for: Berlin was exciting. Berlin was cheap. Berlin was as hedonistic as it had been in the 1920s. Berlin was already over. Berlin had not yet begun. I would love Berlin.

I listened to as much advice as I could take, and then ignored most of it. I knew all the while that, although it might help me, each opinion I listened to could shape my experience of the city before I had even gotten there and had a chance to make it my own. Friends told me to move to Friedrichshain, to

Old meets new in Berlin's Regierungsviertel >

live in Prenzlauer Berg, that I would love Kreuzberg. I listened to none of them and found my first flatshare somewhere else. I was bombarded with all manner of helpful advice on how to learn German, how to avoid falling into the trap of associating only with English speakers—or worse still, only Americans. I cannot say that I consciously followed any of it—and neither should you.

I urge you to use this book in much the same way I used all that friendly advice. Page through it for inspiration. Lean on it to assuage your fears and fuel your dreams. Use it as a companion, but don't assume it possesses the power to dictate exactly what your experience of moving to Berlin will be, or that it can tell you exactly how to live once you get here. Berlin is changing so fast these days (then again, that's what they said five, ten, and 20 years ago), you may find it difficult to keep up, even with the help of a book such as this one. Embrace it.

Berlin is exciting. Berlin is still comparatively cheap. Berlin has many sides, some of them as hedonistic as they were in the 1920s. Berlin is already over. Berlin has not yet begun. You will love Berlin.

WELCOME TO BERLIN

Much like that famous Winston Churchill quote about Russia, Berlin can often seem like a "riddle wrapped in a mystery inside an enigma." To young first-timers, it may seem impossible that a city this vibrant, this central, and this cosmopolitan could still be so cheap. To those who were born here, or perhaps have lived here for a good portion of their lives, it can be perplexing and somewhat laughable that anyone would care about this place: Berlin, after all, spent much of its life as a somewhat provincial outpost just within the borders of several great empires—before finding itself at the center of 20th century history. To everyone else, Berlin is simply a fascinating and bewildering place that, even in the years since its reunification, somehow seems to live outside the boundaries of normal time and space.

It's quickly catching up on all counts, though, and visitors these days will find a city both thoroughly wrapped up in itself and embracing of all outsiders, a city where deep construction holes and swiftly rising ultra-modern buildings are just as common as old mainstay neighborhoods that don't appear to have changed in a century, a city where a student can feel just as at home as an artist, or a high-powered politician, or a retiree, as long as he doesn't take himself too seriously. The ubiquitous quote from Berlin's longtime mayor Klaus Wowereit, that the city is "poor but sexy" has probably been used to sell everything from guidebooks to T-shirts by now, but those repeating it often ignore the greater significance of it: it is not the words that Wowereit (or "Wowi," as he is known to his supporters) chose to use, but rather the fact that he said them at all: that even the mayor of a European capital is comfortable enough with his hometown to label it in such a way, and to be reasonably certain of no resulting backlash. Most would agree with him: Berlin has been penniless for far too long. But like many a penniless artist, its lack of money has forced it to get creative in other ways.

BERLIN IN THE 21ST CENTURY

Berlin nowadays is a city still coming into its own, in more ways than one. In 1991, two years after the fall of the Berlin Wall and only one year after official reunification, the German parliament voted, by an extremely small margin, to make Berlin the capital of reunified Germany. (During the divided years, Berlin had been the capital of East Germany, while the West German capital was moved to Bonn.) Ask many German politicians today, and publicly they'll tell you that it was a good decision, but privately, perhaps they're still struggling with it. Although the impressive, modern Regierungsviertel (government quarter) has come to define "new Berlin," many politicians forced to work there may still long for their genteel homes in the south. In fact, the conventional cliché is that many still have homes there, staying in Berlin only as long as it takes to vote and attend a couple of high-powered luncheons, and then high-tailing it back to the other side of the Rhine. Now, with the addition of the Bundesnachrichtendienst, Germany's central intelligence agency, entire city blocks at the northern edge of Mitte, Berlin's central district, have been overhauled. A barren stretch of the city has now been enlivened with shops, hotels, and cafés, all intended to service a swarm of government agents.

In addition, companies that jumped ship when the Wall went up, abandoning the city after the war for the southern regions that were safer for business interests, are returning. Once again, Berlin is proving itself ripe for business and industry, and nothing has reflected this trend more strongly than it's emergence as the so-called "Silicon Allee," the German home of international startups. In just the last five years, Berlin has been flooded with startup offices, some of them the European headquarters of companies that have already found a measure of success elsewhere, others merely German versions of already successful ideas. Most of these companies are relentlessly international, hiring employees from many parts of the world who speak many languages and have decidedly 21st century talents, like coding and social media expertise. In many ways, Berlin is the perfect city for startups, as the Berlin lifestyle and the startup lifestyle fit each other so well: both are laid back, unconventional, and value creative drive and innovation over long but less productive working hours. It's no great shock that Berlin and Silicon Valley have become fast friends; it's only surprising that it didn't happen sooner.

Add to that the fact that every year, Berlin is flooded with students and artists, the former attracted by essentially free educations offered at multiple top universities, technical colleges, and trade schools, the latter lured in by the still relatively cheap rent and the buzz of creativity fueled by it. If a comparison must be made between Berlin and some other city, think of New York in the 80s, minus the crime. The historical explanation for Berlin's low rents will be discussed later, but suffice it to say, they've been enough to give every artist, musician, or writer who might have been discouraged by the cost of living in most other cities a chance at some level of success here. With rents for studios or co-working spaces still only a couple of hundred Euros a month, and living costs still well under a thousand a month depending on the neighborhood, artists can afford to get creative without sacrificing precious time and energy on a boring day job. The dearth of drive, however, and the lack of a true challenge to overcome has its advantages and disadvantages. While some truly embrace the open, effortless lifestyle Berlin provides, others find the lack of outside pressure to succeed dulls their ambition, making it difficult to reach goals, much less set them in the first place. It is as if the entire city, having been bombed to shreds in WWII, has decided to remake itself not once, not twice, but over and over again. And its inhabitants, taking their cues from the city itself, have decided that the best way to live there is simply to follow suit.

It is hard to say whether Berlin attracts a certain type of person, or whether those who move here become that type after a certain amount of time, but as you navigate the neighborhoods and face the faces of this ever-changing city, you'll find that those who choose to make it their home are of the most unconventional sort. Welcome to their midst; you are now one of them. Berlin today may be the seat of government, it may have several major universities, but really, it is the perfect blend of history and creativity that makes Berlin what it is today: perhaps not just a great 21st century city, but a model for what 21st century cities should be.

BERLIN HISTORY IN A NUTSHELL

Many, if not most, newly-minted Berliners are young enough not to remember the Berlin Wall, and for many of them those tumultuous, heady days when the Wall fell, taking Communism and the Eastern Bloc down with it, are only a vague recollection. So newcomers can often arrive with an embarrassingly limited knowledge of what Berlin was like before they got there. This is a shame, as having some idea of Berlin's history can be crucial to understanding and appreciating it.

Starting from the beginning would fill a book on its own, but the most relevant recent history, and the story that makes for the most compelling reading, starts towards the beginning of the 20th century. Berlin started right where the city still looks its oldest, at the area where the Spree River parts to encircle Museum Island, where the Nikolaiviertel and the Fischerinsel still charm with their reconstructed period buildings. Two settlements—Berlin and Cölln—merged to form what would first be part of the Margravate of Brandenburg (still the name of the region surrounding Berlin today), then the capital of Prussia, and much later the center of the German Empire.

By the end of WWI, Berlin was still the capital, but it was hanging on by a thread due to overcrowding, lack of coal, and the simple fact that it was at the center of a defeated empire, now no longer a monarchy but a republic—the so-called Weimar Republic. Although the interwar years are the ones Berliners tend to wax nostalgic about (though few are still alive today who could remember them), the Roaring Twenties and the Golden Age they were not, but rather an exuberant, topsy-turvy, dangerous world of excess, "divinely decadent" as the inimitable Sally Bowles, star of the Christopher Isherwood novel *Goodbye to Berlin* that would later become the musical *Cabaret*, would have it. Here, Communists and Nazis clashed in the streets, the value of the German *Reichsmark* soared, and Jews, homosexuals, Roma people, and other so-called "undesirables" first began to suspect that their world was collapsing. But it was also a whirlwind of creativity, producing some of Germany's greatest works of art, literature, music, and theater.

Still, high unemployment, exorbitant reparation payments (which caused inflation in the first place, as the German government frantically printed money and borrowed in order to pay back the victorious allies), and a feeling of an old order and a highly prized culture slipping away may have first led the public to vote Hitler: in just a few years, he went from a far right nuisance many assumed would not gain ground to the chancellor of Germany; a country very quickly losing its status as a free-thinking republic. By the time Hitler invaded Poland in 1939, things had already devolved quite rapidly for Berlin and its citizens. While it was of course the Jews who felt the brunt of it, even a full-fledged "aryan" who didn't blend into the background by following the rules or dared to express anything but full support for the Nazis could quickly find himself under suspicion—or worse.

After the war destroyed any traces of Berlin the Nazis had not already ruined, it was left a bombed out shell of its former self. The remains were divided among four victorious powers: America, Britain, France, and Russia. This division reflected a division of power along the same lines nationwide, with each country taking over a section of Germany along with Berlin. Berlin, of course, was in a uniquely precipitous position as Russia began to exert greater power over the Soviet Occupied Zone. By 1949, after withdrawing from the council of allied powers that governed occupied Germany, Russia proceeded to form its own satellite nation of East Germany, with East Berlin as its capital. This left West Berlin, by name still a part of West Germany, an island of capitalism in the midst of an increasingly hostile communist state.

That hostility came to a head in 1948, when the Soviets sealed off access to West Berlin in an attempt to besiege the city and take it for themselves. In one of the allies' first postwar triumphs, which would cement America and Britain as valuable

The ruins of the Kaiser-Wilhelm-Gedächtniskirche (memorial church) >

friends instead of occupying powers in the minds of a generation of Germans, airplanes manned by practically every member of the English-speaking world (America, Britain, Canada, Australia, New Zealand, South Africa) delivered all the supplies needed to sustain West Berlin and its people by air. Tempelhof airport, built in the 1920s but redesigned during Hitler's time as a symbol of Nazi power, would act as the gateway for the Berlin airlift or *Luftbrücke* ("air bridge"), becoming a symbol of Berlin's postwar resilience in the face of a new threat.

It was not only this failed power grab that left East Germany feeling the crush of defeat, however; due to ever-harsher economic conditions in their sector, East Germans were increasingly leaving their homes and crossing through East Berlin into West Berlin and from there into the rest of West Germany where, they hoped, a more prosperous future awaited them. After failing to convince the newly-minted East Germans it was in their best interests to stay, the government employed another tactic in 1961: practically overnight, the Berlin Wall was built, dividing a city that was already divided, deepening a wound that was now completely, horrifyingly permanent.

In the coming years, over a hundred desperate people would be either killed or wounded trying to breech the Berlin Wall. Families would be torn apart, neighborhoods would be ripped in two as entire buildings were demolished—sometimes rental houses occupied by normal people, occasionally even historical churches, their steeples toppled in one fell swoop—to make way for the death strip and its impressive array of traps and alarms. With its many monuments, museums, and the touristy Checkpoint Charlie recreation, the Berlin of today sometimes seems fixated on turning the years between 1961 and 1989 into a James Bond film—or at least a John le Carré novel. And while the history of the Berlin Wall is no doubt one of the 20th century's most intriguing, a spy story of epic proportions around which the fate of the world seemed to revolve, it is also, at its core, profoundly sad.

Postwar West Berlin would continue to grow and thrive, mostly thanks to an overwhelming influx of capital from the rest of the country. The city-state that was no longer the capital of its own country but sort of an entire country of its own—an island nation in the midst of troubled waters—would be turned into a destination for arts and culture, fueled by tax money, the youngest, most daring members of the population, and an ongoing reputation as something of a refuge for those who didn't belong. A perpetual sense of dread hung in the air: the very real threat that the Russians would once again try to block the city's connection to the outside world or invade it directly made it very difficult for established companies to risk setting up a headquarters there. Those who could, moved, and took Berlin's industrial potential with them. Likewise, to West Germans living anywhere else, benefitting from an economy on the upswing, dubbed the *Wirtschaftswunder* (economic wonder), nothing could be farther from the radar than their former capital. So rents stayed cheap, the establishment stayed out for the most part, and Berlin became the ultimate paradox: a metropolis coasting along on its own underdog status while the fate of the Western world seemed to rest on its shoulders.

Then the Berlin Wall fell, and Berliners rejoiced over a miracle they hadn't dared to hope for in their lifetimes. But once the party was over, the two countries were left to pick up their many pieces and paste them together, somewhat haphazardly, into what would become a new Germany...again. In many ways that experiment is still underway, as Berlin explores what kind of a city it wants to be and its inhabitants enjoy a certain influence they might not have in other cities. Because they are here, now, they have a hand in crafting a city that still has yet to truly become one.

UNDERSTANDING THE BERLIN MENTALITY

Although every city-dweller nurtures a feeling of pride, of "I was there when...," Berlin's unique history makes it a special case. Shortly after moving here, you'll probably find it difficult to keep track of the number of times you've been subjected to stories about the night the Wall fell (that's November 9, 1989). Some of them will be intriguing enough that you'll want to hear more, others you'll just have to nod politely to, but what you choose to read into these stories will be a pretty accurate gauge of how you react to the Berlin mentality in general. Make no mistake about it, these nostalgic reminiscences can be both entertaining and moving, but they're also meant to put the listener in his place, projecting an attitude that is both insular and welcoming, friendly and testy, and above all, serves to communicate a sense of "having been there" that the newly-minted Berliner can only hope to attain.

This is all a very roundabout way of introducing the concept of *Berliner Schnauze*, which is hardly worth translating, as any direct translation would fail to come close to its actually meaning. It is that sense of attitude with a wink, complaining with one corner of your mouth turned up in a sly smile, rudeness crossed with humor. The cheek you'll sometimes get at Berlin's trendier cafés and restaurants doesn't even come close, for Berlin is so young and international these days, *Berliner Schnauze* has become the domain of the old or at least middle-aged. But they've been through a lot here. Let them keep it.

Of course, what they've been through also has a strong effect on their attitude towards outsiders. Unlike many rapidly changing capitals, where the amount of time one spends there can only really be measured from the day he arrives, Berlin's inhabitants can be divided into two fairly solid categories: those who were there before the Wall fell, and those who weren't. Nowhere else in recent history has an event so affected its people, so the distinction is therefore notable and even necessary. Putting one foot on each side of the thin brick line that memorializes the path of the Wall certainly makes for a good tourist photo. It's something else entirely, though, to remember what those streets actually looked like pre-1989, and to feel the significance of stepping across the greatest of great divides.

Perhaps in a year or two you'll be able to remember things that the current flock of newbies couldn't even imagine: when that towering office building was just a gaping hole, for example, or when a certain neighborhood still felt undiscovered…at least to you. Then you'll know the simultaneous feeling of pain and longing mixed with fascination that must surely greet the native Berliner: he's seen it all, for sure, but he no longer recognizes his own city. The only response to this threat of encroaching change? *Berliner Schnauze*.

BERLIN'S MANY FACES

THE TWELVE OFFICIAL DISTRICTS

Visitors to Berlin may well end up wondering why they didn't choose to move here earlier. Despite the fall of the Berlin Wall over two decades ago, the city still displays a dichotomy that runs along east-west lines. Those who come to Berlin seeking the refinement and sophistication of a world capital may be satisfied or dismayed, depending on where they choose to live. This is why a thorough understanding of Berlin's districts can be extremely valuable. The hedonistic atmosphere of post-1989 Berlin has given way to the upper-middle-class comfort and relaxation of gentrified neighborhoods: those who used to party the night away have since grown up and had children of their own, and their districts have changed along with them. Meanwhile, the old West, once seen as stuffy, is now experiencing a rebirth of its own, as those too old for the student areas but too alternative for the married-with-kids lifestyle seek a third way, renewing classic Berlin neighborhoods as they seek their own renewal.

A little over ten years ago, Berlin's neighborhoods also experienced something of a renewal, albeit only a surface one. Up until 2000, Berlin comprised 23 different *Bezirke* or official districts, each with its own distinctive history and character. Then, in 2001, these 23 were consolidated into twelve, some of which are still shaking their heads in puzzlement, wondering what got them stuck together so arbitrarily. Still, many of the same age-old mentalities remain, while the names seem to serve only government employees (so called *Beamter*) or opportunistic real estate agents. Whether they serve to give you a broader picture of your new home, to inspire you to explore, or simply to confuse you, here are the twelve official districts of Berlin.

MITTE

Your first few days in Berlin will most likely be spent in this district, and indeed it is not hard to guess what "mitte" means, even if you don't speak German. Mitte's energy ranges from staid to bustling to overwhelming, it contains most of the historical sites, hotels, and museums you will find in any guidebook, and nearly all of the noteworthy government buildings, including the Reichstag. It is not only central geographically, but truly in the middle of everything.

Areas: Everything from guidebook-ready (old) Mitte to Moabit, Tiergarten (including the park), and Wedding.

Top attractions: Potsdamer Platz has been built up considerably in the decades since the Wall fell, an approximation of New York's Times Square with its shiny steel skyscrapers. Unter den Linden too is a name on the lips of everyone who first sets foot here, a grand boulevard ending in the Brandenburg Gate and flanked by the American, British, Russian and French embassies. The Scheunenviertel—once a gritty no man's land where Jewish immigrants made their homes, and now some of the most desirable real estate in the city, is full of elegant, immaculately renovated Prussian buildings interspersed with commercial streets offering a mixture of small restaurants, cafés, and boutiques. Farther north in Wedding, the Panke canal, dotted with old industrial buildings turned artist workshops, is the perfect scenic Berlin walkway, and bustling Leopoldplatz sits at the center of one of Berlin's most diverse areas.

Best Kept Secret: Moabit constitutes one of the last true "old Berlin" neighborhoods, seemingly impervious to gentrification, tourism, and trends. On partially cobblestoned, leafy streets, you're bound to pass small businesses that have been around for decades, restaurants with loyal local clientele, and pensioners sitting outside local *Kneipen* (pubs) having a beer at midday. The Hansaviertel, a small *Kiez* or neighborhood within Moabit, was the result of Interbau, an international competition to find architects who would reimagine a neighborhood devastated after WWII. The goal was to create something so new and modern as to rival the bombastic magnificence of Karl-Marx-Allee, then being built in East Berlin. Walking through the Hansaviertel today is a bit of a nostalgia trip, helped by the fact that hardly anyone under the age of sixty seems to live there.

Cost: Quite high to moderate, depending on area. Touristy Mitte has grown to be the most expensive part of the city, while parts of Moabit, Wedding, and Tiergarten still offer comparatively affordable spaces.

FRIEDRICHSHAIN-KREUZBERG

Kreuzberg and Friedrichshain, separated by the Spree river, may be next to each other, but to most of their inhabitants at the time of their union, they were about as different as could be. Now the neighborhoods in this central and highly livable area have grown closer. Both were known as highly alternative just after the Wall fell: Friedrichshain as a longtime worker's quarter, Socialist stronghold, and home to some of the East's most impressive buildings, Kreuzberg sufferered from the blight and isolation caused by being surrounded by the Wall on three sides.

Areas: Friedrichshain consists of Stralau, Oberbaum City, Boxhagener Kiez, and the area around Karl-Marx-Allee, and Kreuzberg consists of two districts known by their old West German postal codes: Kreuzberg 36 (for post code SO36) and Kreuzberg 61 (for post code SW61).

Top Attractions: Connecting the two districts via the Spree is the Oberbaumbrücke, the Disney castle-ish gothic bridge where inhabitants of the two districts meet each other annually in spectacular displays of good-natured rivalry: a water and vegetables fight in summer. The buildings along Karl-Marx-Allee are simultaneously revered and reviled, both for what they represent and for their architectural style, which fascinates many but reminds others of the fascist architecture that characterized Mussolini's reign in Italy. Love it or hate it, one cannot fail to be anything less than bowled over by the endless wide boulevard with Mitte's iconic TV Tower at one end, more reminiscent of Moscow than any city in Germany. Make a point of walking among these so-called *Stalinbauten*, starting at Alexanderplatz and strolling east past other Communist landmarks like the Kino International and the former Karl-Marx-Buchhandlung. Kreuzberg has an abundance of parks, including the shabby and beloved Görlitzer Park, a strip of green that used to be a railroad terminal, the magnificent Viktoriapark with its waterfall and stunning hilltop view, and the new Park am Gleisdreieck, a sprawling collection of playgrounds, community gardens and walkways made out of an old train depot.

Worst Kept Secret: The Landwehrkanal running through Kreuzberg all the way to Neukölln is an idyllic walkway that plays host to one of the city's most beloved outdoor markets, Maybachufer, where Turkish vegetable sellers call out their wares, making for a lively atmosphere slightly reminiscent of Istanbul.

Cost: Once astonishingly low, housing prices have really gone up in recent years, especially in Kreuzberg areas like those around Chamissoplatz, Graefestraße, or the beautifully renovated and newly hip Markthalle IX, an old brick market hall.

TEMPELHOF-SCHÖNEBERG

The district of Tempelhof-Schöneberg is also something of an anomaly. Although the joining of the two might seem strange to their inhabitants, even a born and bred Berliner would now find it difficult to pick out on a map exactly where one ends and the other begins.

Areas: Tempelhof is about as suburban as you're going to get in Berlin. The three green, leafy, and wholly un-urban neighborhoods of Mariendorf, Marienfelde, and Lichtenrade share space with the northern section that borders the former Tempelhof airport (now a park, its runways given over to bikers, skaters, and kite fliers), called the Fliegerviertel (flyer's quarter) for the many airmen and passengers that surely passed through it. Schöneberg contains several tiny and desirable *Kieze*, including the Bayerisches Viertel or Bavarian Quarter, and the areas around Winterfeldtplatz and Akazienstraße. Nollendorfplatz is the traditional heart of gay Berlin, whereas the so-called Rote Insel or "red island" used to be a Communist stronghold. The sleepy neighborhood of Friedenau has some beautiful old buildings and a high concentration of pensioners.

Top Attractions: Schöneberg boasts a substantial number of attractive, old-world squares, like the highly sought-after Vik-

< *Kanuliebe (canoe love) on the Spree between Kreuzberg and Friedrichshain*

toria-Luise-Platz, that feel almost Parisian in their upscale, fountain-trickling elegance, and the bustling Winterfeldtplatz, which hosts one of the city's best outdoor markets every Saturday. Former Schöneberg inhabitants as diverse as David Bowie, Christopher Isherwood, and Marlene Dietrich are almost attractions in themselves. The Fliegerviertel is one of the city's most unexpected quarters: It's tiny, one-lane streets are lined not with apartments, but with two- and three- story standalone and row houses that conceal back gardens.

Best Kept Secret: The Natur-Park Schöneberger Südgelände, an old train depot in the space between two 19th century rail lines, now turned into a sprawling nature reserve where gravel paths crisscross old train tracks and the rusty remnants of industry still peak out above the trees.

Cost: The southern parts of Tempelhof (Marienfelde, etc.) offer mostly single-family properties inhabited by their owners. The Fliegerviertel used to be a true best kept secret, but has now gotten a lot more expensive as people realize they have a chance to live in their own houses while still technically in the city center. Schöneberg has gotten much more expensive as of late as well, with costs now equaling or topping properties in Mitte and Prenzlauer Berg.

NEUKÖLLN

Long on the brink of something, Neukölln finally exploded in popularity about five years ago, and has been on the up and up ever since. Once considered one of the most blighted and dangerous neighborhoods (as it still appears to many who don't live there and would never set foot there), Neukölln is a high-density immigrant area where cheap prices and proximity to Kreuzberg have attracted students, artists, and underdogs since long before its name was on the lips of real estate agents. Though there may not be so much in the way of well-known tourist attractions to lure visitors, do not dismiss this neighborhood simply because it does not yet show up in some guidebooks. Its many *Kieze*, each with its own local flare

The pub Ankerklause *on the Maybachufer at Kottbusser Brücke is a popular spot in all seasons.* >

and proud history, make Neukölln one of Berlin's most livable districts.

Areas: Although it extends quite far south and consists of both inner-city high rises like Gropiusstadt and practically rural farmland along the former German-German border, the area most people talk about when they talk about Neukölln north of the Ringbahn consists of several neighborhoods: Kreuzkölln, the part of Neukölln bordering the idyllic Landwehrkanal, Schillerkiez east of Tempelhof, which has experienced rapid gentrification since the airport became a park, Rixdorf at central Neukölln's southeastern end, and Britz below the Ringbahn.

Top attractions: The pathway along the Landwehrkanal can provide a perfect place for promenading, and the section of the canal next to Kottbusser Brücke is also home to the beloved twice-weekly Maybachufer market. Farther south, the hidden idylls of Körnerpark, the tiny Comeniusgarten and the hills of Thomashöhe and Lessinghöhe (literally: "heights") provide welcome breaks from city life. Several cemeteries flanking Hermannstraße's lower reaches offer a sense of history and weightiness amidst the commercial bustle. Richardplatz, the square at the center of old Rixdorf, formerly a Bohemian

village before being incorporated into Berlin, draws crowds for an old-fashioned Christmas market where revelers drink mulled wine and shop for church crafts by gas lamp light.

Best Kept Secret: Gutshof Britz, a former manor estate that now houses a restaurant by a Michelin-started chef, a wonderful *Heimatmuseum* or local museum with an exhibition of objects representing Neukölln history, and a working farm.

Cost: Although getting up there due to its popularity, Neukölln's southern neighborhoods still offer some very cheap real estate.

PANKOW

One of Berlin's largest districts and its most heterogenous, Pankow stretches to the northernmost border of the city, where quiet suburbs centered around S-Bahn stations feel almost rural. At its southern end, Pankow is thoroughly urban.

Areas: The dense neighborhoods of Prenzlauer Berg, Weißensee, and Pankow are closer to Berlin's center, while farther north the areas of Heinersdorf, Blankenfelde, Blankenburg, Karow, Malchow, Buch, Französisch Buchholz, Niederschönhausen, and Rosenthal are more like clusters of villages than real city districts.

Top attractions: Prenzlauer Berg stands out more for its reputation than for any one of its neighborhoods: over the last decade or so, it has been repeatedly trumpeted in the media as the one exception to sinking German fertility rates. Like it or not, sooner or later you'll probably have an opinion about Prenzlauer Berg. Disparaged by older locals as a gentrification travesty, proof that West Germans who quickly moved in after reunification merely destroyed every ounce of character it had left, Prenzlauer Berg has a lot of controversy brewing under its cobblestone streets, kid-friendly cafés, and stroller-filled squares. True, a lot of the East Germans who were here when the Wall fell were quickly disenfranchised, unable to buy the crumbling houses they had lived in for decades because they came with hefty price tags in the form of renovation contracts (practically collapsing buildings, for example, went for very little at governmental auctions, as long as the buyers promised to sink a fortune into their reparation). But other Berlin neighborhoods have seen much the same; a general trending towards young families taking over while the elderly move on.

Weißensee is one place where time seems to have stood still. At its center is the eponymous lake and at its southernmost corner stands the largest Jewish cemetery in all of Europe. Until recently, the neighborhood of Pankow seemed to have somehow missed the gentrification wave. In the last few years, however, fueled by demand from those priced out of Prenzlauer Berg, Pankow has become known for the highest concentration of building projects in the city. Centered on Breite Straße, its main shopping street, Pankow was always a bit too far from the excitement of the center. But now it's catching on with families in a big way, who see the district, with its many small green spaces like the Bürgerpark, Schlosspark, and Volkspark Schönholzer Heide, as a perfect, low-key place to raise kids.

Best Kept Secrets: The Volkspark Prenzlauer Berg (an actual *Berg* or hill) not only makes for excellent sledding in winter; it is also home to a vineyard growing Berlin's very own Riesling. The winemakers also offer actual wine tours.

At its northern end, where Prenzlauer Berg bleeds into Pankow, squat, square buildings in the Bauhaus style from the 1930s are like a glimpse into the past. They may have been given a new coat of paint here and there, but now they can seem even older to the casual passerby than the gleaming pastels of the perfectly restored *Altbau* buildings further south.

Cost: Quite high in the south, especially since this district has become a magnet for well-to-do families and successful professionals. Still pleasantly low in the north, which is so far from the center as to feel almost like the countryside.

CHARLOTTENBURG-WILMERSDORF

When people think of West Berlin in its heyday, the scenes that come to mind probably took place on the streets of this region, made up of two upscale districts united into one. Both have an especially high concentration of cultural institutions. Charlottenburg is home to its opera house, theaters, and universities: the Technische Universität (TU) and the Universität der Künste (UdK), one of Germany's premier universities for the arts.

Areas: Charlottenburg's southern areas includes Kurfürstendamm or Ku'damm, the traffic heavy area around Zoologischer Garten and the genteel Savignyplatz, while its northern end includes the Schloss Charlottenburg and a more gritty, industrial area. Wilmersdorf is characterized by several busy boulevards and some truly lovely squares. Grunewald is probably the most expensive, upscale residential district in the city. On the outskirts, Schmargendorf and Westend house some of the city's older, upper-class residents.

Top attractions: This region has a relatively high percentage of non-German residents, leading to some of the best international cuisine in Berlin. The influx of Russian immigrants when the Wall fell led to the nickname "Charlottengrad" for Charlottenburg, whether affectionate or not, while the number of authentic Asian restaurants on and around Kantstraße has led to it becoming a sort of mini-Asiatown. The expansive shopping boulevard Ku'damm runs down the district's center. The area around Ludwigkirchplatz in Wilmersdorf is full of upscale shops, fancy cafés, and some of the most decorative *Altbau* buildings in Berlin, while Savignyplatz also offers gawking opportunities and envy-inducing real estate. Of course, Charlottenburg's northern end is capped by the most envious bit of real estate in town: the magnificent Schloss Charlottenburg, a Prussian palace that was once the royal residence of the Hohenzollern and named after Sophie Charlotte, wife of Friedrich I. Today, the Schloss is a museum, its gorgeous grounds a public park. Farther afield is Lietzensee, a lake perfect for boating in summer and ice-skating in winter.

The Grunewald neighborhood in the southwest is so distinctive it should be its own district. A gigantic park with several lakes, a man-made hill (Teufelsberg), and even its own *Jagdschloss* (hunting lodge), bordered by street after street of upscale villas, this is another area to dream and get lost in.

Worst Kept Secret: The popularity of the so-called "Thai Park," a gathering of Southeast Asian families cooking authentic dishes in Wilmersdorf's Preußenpark on warm weekends has further served to give Berliners a different view of their city.

Vibe: In recent years, fueled by a spate of development around Zoologischer Garten (the infamous Zoo Station, which was at its grungiest and druggiest in the '70s and '80s and has since

^ *Partly Charlottenburg, partly Zehlendorf: the city forest Grunewald*

moved on only partially) the "cool factor" of this neighbor-hood has risen somewhat, luring more of the young, hip Berlin residents who might have chosen Mitte just a few years ago. The recent construction of the towering Waldorf-Astoria hotel caused quite a commotion, signaling the revival of this district as a formidable Mitte rival, while the sleek and modern Bikini Berlin shopping center acts as a calling card for this old, new district. The impending opening of the beloved C/O Gallery, which moved into the down-and-out Amerika-Haus adjacent to Zoo, has been taken as all the evidence necessary to signal that the West is back.

Cost: Quite high overall, especially around Savignyplatz and Ludwigkirchplatz.

TREPTOW-KÖPENICK

Follow the Spree southeast, and you'll eventually end up in this district, by far Berlin's largest while at the same time the least populated, owing to its high concentration of parks, woods, and waterways. This area can sometimes feel a bit sleepy at first, but it is also immensely intriguing, as if hidden history were seeping through every crack. Stick around long enough and you may not only discover its secrets; you may come to love its proximity to both city and country, its higher concentration of "real" old Berliners, and its undiscovered quality.

Areas: Farther north, the districts of Treptow and Plänterwald are intensely green. Moving east, industrial Oberschöneweide and Niederschöneweide flank the Spree. Köpenick has its own historical old town, and visiting Grünau and Friedrichshagen feels a bit like traveling back in time. Adlershof has gotten a reputation for its tech and scientific campuses.

Top attractions: The forest-like Treptower Park offers enough attractions to fill days worth of wandering. You'll most likely find yourself here for the first time to go picnicking by the river, where houseboats form a nice little colony of their own, or to see the impossibly huge and wonderfully bombastic

Russian memorial (Sowjetisches Ehrenmal), which was built soon after WWII to honor the Russian sacrifice in the "Great War." Drive or bike down Pushkinallee or Am Treptower Park to see some prime examples of eastern real estate: proud villas, every bit as grand as those in Grunewald, hold their own against their West Berlin counterparts. The old town of Köpenick, which gave its name to the district, located on a little spit of land where the Spree meets the Dahme river, was once its very own village. Its charming historic area with a *Schloss* and local *Rathaus* (city hall) makes for a nice half-day jaunt. Friedrichshagen is one of the best places to access the Müggelsee, the largest lake in Berlin proper. The now-defunct Berliner Bürgerbräu, the oldest brewery in the area, is still an impressive site from the south side of the river as well. Rahnsdorf offers an enchanting collection of canals known as Neu-Venedig (New Venice).

Worst Kept Secret: In the Plänterwald, an equally large green space next to Treptower Park, rests an attraction that has lured thrill-seekers for years: Spreepark, an abandoned amusement park with a long and sordid history. Although breaking into it has become something of a rite-of-passage, nowadays it's easier just to go on an official tour or wait for a music festival to take place there. The city of Berlin recently bought back this enchanted site, but Berliners will have to wait a few more years (or maybe a decade in Berlin time) to see how the story ends

Best Kept Secret: The sprawling Funkhaus Nalepastraße complex in Oberschöneweide was once home to East German radio and is still very much in use—both by recording artists taking advantage of the superior sound studios and by visual artists who rent out small atelier rooms and galleries in the main building.

Cost: Still quite reasonable; prices go even lower as you head farther east.

STEGLITZ-ZEHLENDORF

More a collection of villages than a city district, this area is tailor-made for those who value privacy, relaxation, and calmness—and who want more space than an apartment can provide. Much like any small, intellectual college town, Dahlem (home to the Freie Universität, FU) seems to exist in a bubble all its own, full of tiny, quaint streets with a library or museum on every corner.

Areas: Steglitz, the district's more urban half, presses up against Schöneberg southern end, and offers some of the most *bürgerlich* or conventionally West German middle class living in Berlin. Its main street Schloßstraße offers a mixture of small neighborhood *Konditoreien* (traditional German pastry manufacturers and cafés), conventional chain stores, and a couple of mammoth shopping centers. Zehlendorf is full of parks, lakes, and quiet spots, some of which remain the most beloved summer destinations within city limits. The southernmost section of Grunewald, including the lakes Wannsee, Schlachtensee, Nikolassee and Krumme Lanke, is part of this district, as is Dahlem.

Top Attractions: In fact, most tourists end up here for one thing only: the Dahlem state museums, including the Ethnological Museum (primarily about pre-industrial, non-European cultures), the Museums of Asian Art, and the Museum of European Cultures. Dahlem boasts the 43-hectare Botanischer Garten, which is of course stunning in spring and summer, but can be even more welcoming in winter, when its cactus- and tropical vine-filled greenhouses serves as a happy reminder of the warm weather's eventual return. Even further southwest, the Pfaueninsel (Peacock Island), located in the region of Wannsee but actually on the Havel River, was built by Friedrich Wilhelm II of Prussia as a place to cavort with his mistress in a small castle, garden, and dairy. Today it is still reachable only by boat. Also in Wannsee is the Max Liebermann Villa, former home of the Jewish-German Impressionist painter, and the Haus der Wannsee-Konferenz (House of the Wannsee Conference), which stands as a memorial to Nazi atrocities and contains a moving exhibit about the darkest chapter in German history.

Vibe: A proper West Berlin district, Steglitz-Zehlendorf includes a fairly large percentage of people with high incomes who own their own houses and apartments. Therefore, expect to find a much lower percentage of rental properties than in many other districts, accompanied by higher prices. Most of this area was far enough from the Berlin Wall to remain, if not untouched by it, at least relatively able to ignore its existence. Tucked away in its own little corner, it managed to avoid much of the bombing that devastated the center. Expect to see quite a large number of pre-war buildings in comparatively good shape, passed down by families through the ages.

Cost: Very high, especially in the areas around the lakes in Grunewald and Dahlem with their abundance of grand villas. More reasonable in Steglitz.

REINICKENDORF

As far as outer Berlin districts go, this one is a bit mix-and-match, its housing stock and inhabitants the most diverse, its

< *At the garden of the Max Liebermann Villa, former home of the Jewish-German Impressionist painter*

reputation fairly low profile, when anyone speaks of it at all. Reinickendorf can sometimes feel a bit empty, however, with concentrated business districts around S- and U-Bahn stations giving way to more spread out, less developed streets dotted with residential buildings and industrial yards. Still, a full fifth of it comprises woods and water, a notable luxury for a region that is still so very close to the city center, and the high percentage of fairly low-cost single-family homes makes it a good place to raise kids.

Areas: The largest and most well-known part is Tegel, followed by lesser known regions of Hermsdorf, Heiligensee, Konradshöhe, Frohnau, Wittenau, and Waidmannslust that are more villages of their own than city neighborhoods, full of stately villas and modest country homes. Lübars possesses a time-travel charm similar to Alt-Tegel, with a concentration of farms and horse stables, and Märkisches Viertel has the first large residential colony or *Großsiedlung* in West Berlin.

Top attractions: Tegel Airport, if you can call it an attraction, is the central, convenient airport where so many Berliners-to-be make first contact with the city. Although the airport's closure due to the opening of the new Berlin-Brandenburg International (BBI) may still be a ways away (in true Berlin fashion, BBI's opening date has been pushed back and back, in a political quagmire that has surprised absolutely no one), its planned transformation into a technology campus should surely bring a jolt of life and some new jobs to the area. Alt-Tegel, the historical center at the northern end of the U6 line, where many a puzzled traveler has no doubt ended up thinking it was the airport, is indisputably lovely, with cobblestone streets and old houses encircling a church at its center, all leading to a promenade along Tegeler See, the second biggest Berlin lake. Large enough for water-skiers, sailboats, and swimmers to share, Tegeler See is also close enough to the city center that it can get quite packed on hot summer days. Farther south, the Hallen am Borsigturm are a cluster of red-brick structures that used to make up the Borsigwerke factory, now reimagined as a shopping complex.

Best Kept Secret: Tegel's Russian Orthodox Church and Cemetery is a historical oddity in the middle of an industrial stretch. The church's blue-painted onion domes are especially stunning against the backdrop of golden trees in autumn, and a walk among the ornate headstones is a lovely, fairytale-like break from city life.

Cost: The neighborhoods closer to the center can be quite reasonable, whereas those further north like Frohnau tend to get up there in price thanks to what they offer: genteel upper middle class living with proximity to the big city.

SPANDAU

If you've heard of Spandau before arriving here, you're either an unapologetic Berlin fanatic spending far too much time on research, or you remember British one-hit-wonders from the '80s. True, while those who visit the area in search of the inspiration for Spandau Ballet are bound to be disappointed by its small-town charm (without a sign of new wave music), those who decide to live there will quickly find themselves identifying far more easily as Spandauers than Berliners: Up until 1920, Spandau was still its own city—and an industrial powerhouse at that. Then, much like Rixdorf or the old town of Köpenick, it was incorporated into the city of Berlin. Unlike Rixdorf and Köpenick, however, it never really completed its transformation, and today it feels much more like Berlin's neighboring town than a full-fledged part of it. Although the area that would one day come to be known as Spandau was settled even earlier than Berlin (and most Spandauers are quick to mention their earlier origins proudly), again like many west German cities, its buildings and streets can actually seem newer to the casual passerby. This is due to a massive overhaul in 1978; a program of refurbishment and renovation that left the old town spick and span—and perhaps sadly, a bit sanitized. Every house has been brought back to its prewar glory, and the pedestrian-only shopping zone really makes visitors feel like they've taken a full leap across the Rhine rather than just a simple S- or U-Bahn ride.

Areas: In addition to central Spandau, this district includes Hakenfeld and its Spandauer Forst or forest, and the so-called Wasserstadt Oberhavel, an ambitious building project meant to make the most of an area full of waterways. Just next to it is the area of Staaken, which first gained notoriety as a producer of zeppelins and bombers (post-WWI, when Germany was forbidden from manufacturing such things, the factory was turned into a film studio). The areas of Gatow and Kladow unfold on the western banks of the Havel river farther south, offering some pretty luxurious living for those wishing to forsake the hustle and bustle of Berlin.

Top attractions: As every good German town should, the *Altstadt* of Spandau has its own brick *Rathaus* (city hall), main church St. Nikolai, and even a *Zitadelle* (citadel) for good measure, a veritable cultural destination in its own right: in addition to hosting performances from musical acts like Bob Dylan, the citadel also boasts one of the weirdest attractions in the entire city: a bat-filled basement known as the *Fledermauskeller*.

Best kept secret: Call it the Detroit of Berlin: Siemensstadt was an entire city-within-a-city, built up by Siemens for its factories and workers, a veritable live-work paradise for Siemens employees complete with its own railway (now defunct), the Siemensbahn. Today, its ranks have thinned considerably, and walking around is like an adventure through a post-industrial semi-ghost town, with brick factory buildings lying in wait on placid canals…until, perhaps, they too are transformed, snapped up by Berliners looking for the next undiscovered neighborhood.

Cost: Quite low in and around the neighborhood of Spandau, much higher in the Havel area with its upscale villages.

LICHTENBERG

A viable option for those already priced out of Friedrichshain, this district is just beginning to get over its rough-and-tumble reputation. There was a time not long ago when the name alone could strike fear into the hearts of Germans and non-Germans alike, conjuring up images of anonymous, tombstone-like *Plattenbau* eyesores (modern high-rise rentals) housing down-and-out characters barely aware that the Berlin Wall had even fallen, along with a narrow-minded atmosphere quite hostile to foreigners. It would be dishonest to say that the area has undergone a complete turnaround in the last few years, but it would also be quite unfair to lean entirely on well-worn clichés. Lichtenberg, created out of the original districts of Lichtenberg and Hohenschönhausen, can seem unwelcoming at first. Most Berliners only get an impression of Lichtenberg as they zoom down Landsberger Allee. That's a shame. From this boulevard, the area's major thoroughfare, the view can look pretty bleak: miles and miles of those high-rise apartment buildings, seemingly repeating each other endlessly like some kind of Tetris tessellation punctuated by the occasional shopping center or big box store. But bear in mind that another Lichtenberg exists behind this concrete curtain: a mixture of small-villages with their own old-timey charm, residential colonies with distinctive early 20th century flourishes, villas both old and new, and enough classic *Altbau* homes to satisfy even the most picky Berlin purist.

Areas: To the north, Alt-Hohenschönhausen seems much like bordering Weißensee: old and new architecture mixes with old and new people, some of them families looking for more space, others wry pensioners who have seen it all, from the Second World War to the rise and fall of the Wall. Lichtenberg proper extends just east of Friedrichshain, and the area surrounding Rummelsburger Bucht, actually a small inlet of the Spree river separated from the rest of it by the Alt-Stralau peninsula (which is a part of Friedrichshain), has been heavily built up over the last few years, with endless rows of rather displaced-looking modern townhouses. The so-called Victoriastadt just east of Ostkreuz is one of the area's best surprises: a 19th century workers' quarter full of *Altbau* buildings with small workshops hidden in their courtyards.

Top attractions: Two lakes (Orankesee and Obersee) in Hohenschönhausen offer enough green space to satisfy locals, while a number of gigantic sports centers join with Sportver-

eine or sports clubs to draw in athletes and those keen on the outdoors. The Tierpark, at 160 hectares one of the largest zoos in the world, features animals from six continents. In the nearby Falkenberg is another notable address for animal-lovers: Europe's largest animal home and clinic, a good place to start when looking to adopt a pet. Meanwhile neighboring Karlshorst, quite an upscale neighborhood that even once earned the moniker "Dahlem of the East," has an impressive horseback riding complex complete with racing track. A bit of exploration will also reveal abandoned factories and industrial complexes ripe for exploring. It can be hard to mention Hohenschönhausen without touching on one of its most important memorial museums: the Gedenkstätte Berlin-Hohenschönhausen. During the Wall years, the spot where it sits was often indicated on East German maps simply by a blank space: that is because, until the Wall fell, it was the site of East Berlin's most notorious prison, where the East German Secret Police, the so-called *Stasi*, deposited anyone and everyone they deemed to have broken the law. For offences so trivial they seem almost comical today, thousands were interrogated, tortured, and locked up. Today, some of them are still tour guides through this monumental prison complex.

Best kept secret: One of the strangest bits of traveling you'll ever do in Berlin may be to the Dong Xuan Center, a collection of huge, stand-alone industrial halls full of cheap Asian gro-

^ *Beauty in the ruins: Even a graffiti covered underpass becomes a place for a stroll in Berlin's Alt-Stralau neighborhood.*

cers and dealers on Hertzbergstraße that attest to the former East's large Vietnamese population.

Cost: Still very low but rising in Lichtenberg, extremely low farther east, where neighborhoods become more spread out and transportation options get sparser.

MARZAHN-HELLERSDORF

Today, this formerly eastern district can still seem cut off from the rest of the world, and even from the rest of Berlin's residents, who are less likely to set foot there than any other district in the city. Unfortunately, a lot of the clichés are still true: along with Lichtenberg, Marzahn-Hellersdorf has one of the highest concentration of radical right (neo-Nazi) residents, a problem the district is working hard to combat with after-school programs and job incentives for young people designed to keep them away from boredom and out of harm's way. A large percentage (nearly two-thirds) of the area's residents live in so-called Plattenbau high-rises, some of which have been renovated and modernized, and many of which have been out-fitted to make "barrier-free" apartments for senior citizens.

Areas: Apart from its high-rises, the southern neighborhoods of Biesdorf, Kaulsdorf, and Mahlsdorf offer comfortable living in single-family houses. These village-like areas come complete with old churches, farmhouses, and cemeteries, seemingly quite far from the stark anonymity of the district's northern half.

Worst kept secret: The Erholungspark Marzahn contains the famed Gärten der Welt (Gardens of the World). This collection of gardens dedicated to different non-western cultures (Chinese, Japanese, Balinese) first started life as part of the Bundesgartenschau (Federal Garden Show) in 1987 and then remained as a retreat for the area's travel-starved residents, who couldn't leave the eastern bloc to actually see any of these places.

Cost: Extremely low, as the area is arguably the least desirable in Berlin.

Picking a neighborhood is a crucial decision for most Berliners, some of whom take it so seriously that they may move every few years, trying out different neighborhoods as if sampling the goods from different bakeries. It's gotten considerably more difficult to flit around the city than it used to be, but you still can and perhaps should, as the area you live in will greatly affect how you perceive the city, not to mention your overall level of life satisfaction. The last thing a new Berliner wants, especially after picking up and moving here, sacrificing familiarity to take a big risk, is to feel he or she has ended up in a place that simply isn't right.

Most new Berliners, especially non-German ones, will probably want to stick to the more international neighborhoods. These days Mitte is probably the safest bet for new arrivals, as it is remains the best connected, the most international, and has the highest concentration of English speakers. Order in English in any Mitte café and you will be understood and served without hesitation. Until recently, Prenzlauer Berg was the second stop for newcomers due to its proximity to Mitte and its status as one of the first former East Berlin neighborhoods to be fully gentrified and colonized—first by so-called Wessis or West Germans, and later by foreigners. Today, it is still one of Berlin's safest districts, but it can also feel a bit too homogenous. In the beginning, Friedrichshain was the alternative, where people liked to move if they wanted a taste of the former East aside from Prenzlauer Berg. It still has pockets of punk, and the atmosphere is still decidedly more anti-establishment, but today Friedrichshain is well on its way to becoming another Prenzlauer Berg, albeit with an alternative reputation to uphold.

Kreuzberg and Neukölln have always attracted a high number of Turkish immigrants, many of whom first came to West Germany as guest workers and stayed (leading to many social questions and problems, both real and imagined—but that's a story for another time). While Kreuzberg was always a magnet for young people—both German and non—looking to live out the fantasy of an alternative, anarchic lifestyle, Neukölln has really exploded in popularity in the past few years, becoming a prime destination for English speakers. While the main streets of Neukölln may look to be straight-up Turkish, the population there is actually a mixture of several Middle Eastern countries.

Wedding continues to have a partially undeserved reputation for drugs, street crime, and general grit. In addition to its Turkish residents, Wedding also plays host to a large percentage of African immigrants. Mixed in with these are your usual smatterings of young Germans and internationals looking for a good deal, who either don't believe the bad reputation or just don't care. You shouldn't either; Wedding is still the most reasonably priced central neighborhood, and offers variety and personality aplenty.

As a general rule, the farther west you go, the older the population gets, and you may actually find yourself running into quite a few Berliners who speak no English at all. While this may seem strange at first in a European capital, keep in mind that many older Berliners simply had no need for the language: they came of age long before the tidal wave of tourists breached their shores, and the language simply was not crucial to their success in a city that still felt predominantly German. Schöneberg seems to have become the district of choice for fairly well to do expats these days. Charlottenburg and Wilmersdorf, as mentioned above, are also getting some of their international pizzazz back, and although the atmosphere is still predominantly German, the many internationals who move there in the coming years will surely change that.

Go further west, into Spandau, Steglitz, or Zehlendorf, and you may feel as if you have left Berlin altogether. After a few years in the city center, however, this can come as a welcome change, and you may find yourself more than thrilled that you have the option to "choose" the big city once a week instead of being thrown headlong into it every day. Internationals may even be welcomed with keener interest here, as they are more rare. Expect a warm reception followed by some polite, friendly questioning.

The city's eastern outskirts, however, are an entirely different beast. As has been hinted earlier, several districts, Lichtenberg and Marzahn-Hellersdorf chief among them, suffer from high unemployment, poverty, and idleness and malaise. This can easily lead to some dire consequences for their social fabric, with many young people joining neo-Nazi groups simply

because they are bored and frustrated. The NPD (Nationalde-
mokratische Partei Deutschlands or German National Democratic Party), basically the modern extension of the Nazi party,
occupies seats in the local governments of both districts as well
as Treptow-Köpenick. This of course lends them a legitimacy
they could not deserve less but still enjoy legally, as Germany
has decided it is better to keep its enemies out in the open than
to ban them outright. For the Berliner who speaks German and
looks European enough to be able to blend in, this can be no
problem at all—but stories abound of non-Westerners, or simply those of slightly darker skin-tone, being followed, harassed,
or even, on occasion, attacked. Again, as with most of Berlin,
these areas are experiencing changes enough that perhaps, in
just a few years, the warning will be wholly unnecessary.

Berlin is, in general, extremely safe. Even in areas that are
regarded as dangerous, which often earn their undeserved
reputations from people who never set foot there, a woman
will probably feel safer than in many other, supposedly better
areas of major European cities. Still, there are a few parks in
town one should avoid after dark, chief among them Hasenheide in Neukölln or Görlitzer Park in Kreuzberg, both of
which are known for their high concentration of drug dealers
and other unsavories completely out in the open, waiting to
make a sale. True, most of the drug dealers in Görlitzer Park
are just down-on-their-luck immigrants trying to make money
the only way they can. They are not to be feared. The drug
scene that grows up around them is what you should watch
out for.

As with any endeavor, what you put into your neighborhood
is what you get out of it. So take the time to explore, pinpoint
that corner bakery where you know you'll be every morning
and introduce yourself. Find out who lives in your building
and when the local town hall meetings take place—as a new-
comer, nothing feels better than having a say in what goes on
around you, and that can be surprisingly easy in Berlin, where
everyone's an activist, and even those who are not can prove
excellent complainers and noise-makers in the right situation.
Even if you only manage to do a couple of these things, it will
go a long way towards making you feel like a real Berliner
through and through.

THE OFFICIAL STUFF

(AND HOW TO GET IT OVER WITH)

There's a reason Germany is well known for its efficiency. The sheer amount of paperwork one must plow through in order to do anything official can be overwhelming. If you come to Berlin as a non-EU citizen, you'll be looking at a distinct disadvantage: you'll have much more to do when you get here. To be German is to expect bureaucracy. For the rest of us, it can come as a bit of a shock. If you find yourself drowning, consider this your life raft.

BERLIN'S *BEAMTEN* – THE MYTH, THE LEGEND, THE REALITY

When navigating your first few months here, you're sure to come across a lot of colorful characters. In contrast, Berlin's famed *Beamten* (government employees) will seem fairly black and white. Feared by Germans and foreigners alike and famous for taking a completely humorless, no-apologies attitude towards the unprepared or ill-informed, *Beamten* act like they know they have a reputation to uphold...as Berlin's biggest sourpusses. You'll hear stories from friends who were rudely dismissed due to a form filled out incorrectly, or who stood on lines in winter before daybreak just to get an appointment. Perhaps even a tale or two of outright rejection. You'll probably believe them, but don't make the mistake of allowing them to turn your nagging doubts into full-blown panic attacks.

Berliners speak of *Beamten* as decidedly average: mostly middle-aged, middle-education, middle-income people who rely on a steady government salary to do very little. Still, what it all comes down to is influence, and Berliners know that, despite the *Beamter*'s middling reputation, he holds a lot of power over each person who comes through his door. That is why, if you listen to a German speak about government officials, you may also detect a hint of envy in their voices. The *Beamter* may be as spießig (square) as can be, but he is the backbone of the city, and for that brief moment when you're sitting in his office, he holds your fate in his hands.

The important thing to remember in every interaction with city officials is that they are only people. *Beamten* can get a bit puffed up by their own importance on occasion, but at the heart of it, they are looking for the same things we all are in our work lives: a bit of respect. Approach them with a modicum of it, and they'll no doubt help you instead of hindering you in what you wish for most: to become an official Berliner, along with all the bureaucracy it entails.

REGISTERING YOUR ADDRESS

A bizarre bit of paperwork that can cost you half an hour or half a day, registering your address will strike you as superfluous at best, downright invasive at worst. Why do it? Well, first of all, the little piece of paper they give you at the end will prove invaluable—as a foreigner, you'll need it to do just about anything else, including signing up for health insurance, opening a bank account, or buying a telephone contract. Second of all, it's the law. As silly as it may seem to you, know that you aren't being discriminated against: this is a bit of bureaucracy even the Germans have to deal with. Third, it will automatically register you with a number of government agencies you will no doubt interact with in the future, all of which will need to be able to send you mail.

The office responsible is the *Einwohnermeldeamt*, which can be found in almost every *Bürgeramt* or district hall. You will need to bring your passport, some cash, and some proof that you live at a certain address. Finally, as with most run-ins with Berlin bureaucracy, even a basic grasp of German can be helpful. You may get lucky with a sympathetic *Beamter* who speaks English, but you'll be just as likely to have to resort to miming in front of a jaded official who is simply over it all. As with many other Berlin services, appointments to register your address can now happily be booked online. Also good to know as it may save time: you can book an appointment at any *Bürgeramt*, regardless of where you live.

Upon arrival, you'll be given a form to fill out and directed to a waiting room. How long you'll have to wait will probably depend on how early you get there. If you have somewhere to be at lunchtime, go at 8, not 11. The form will request your name, birthdate, nationality, and address. It will also ask you to state your religion. Don't panic. This is not for the sake of categorization or discrimination. Germany has elected to collect money for the official Protestant and Catholic churches via a tax on their members. This tax is purely voluntary, since anyone in Germany can self-identify as a tax-paying member of an official church, or deregister when he wishes. This may seem strange and unnecessary to foreigners. But for those who attend church regularly, this is a fairly no-mess, no-fuss way to ensure their tithes are taken care of. If you wish to stay out of the whole thing, check the box marked "other."

Once your number is called, present the form along with your passport and rental contract. If you don't have one, you can usually give them the name of someone on your lease, or at the very least, detailed instructions as to which apartment you live in (floor and wing). Once they have located your address in the system and linked your name to it, they will stamp your slip of paper, called an *Anmeldebestätigung* (registration confirmation) and give you a carbon copy of it. Keep this in a safe place; you will need it again.

HEALTH INSURANCE

Some people who arrive in Germany are a bit disappointed by the state of the healthcare system. Germany does indeed offer public and private options, but those terms can be misleading. Companies offering public health insurance options are obligated to insure everyone who applies regardless of age or pre-existing conditions, and premiums charged are pegged directly to income. If a German company hires you full-time, you are entitled to enroll in a public plan, with your employer paying nearly half your monthly premium. Private health insurance tends to be pricier, and private providers can pick and choose their members, charging astronomical prices for those with pre-existing conditions or refusing to cover them at all. What's more, private insurers tend to up their premiums every year, so even if you start out with a premium you consider fair, ask how much the price is likely to rise annually to get an idea of how much you'll pay when you're sixty.

Private patients enjoy certain advantages, however, including the likelihood of being seen much more quickly by doctors: since doctors are guaranteed payment in full directly from private patients, who must then register their claims to be reimbursed later, they are more inclined to give these patients priority. Public health insurance demands more paperwork from doctors and pays them less. Unfortunately, this leads to a two-tiered system in which those willing to pay private premiums and deal with the hassles of paying out of pocket before being reimbursed will find doctors are more willing to accept them, and more helpful and friendly when treating them. Stories abound of patients trying to make an urgent appointment over the phone in June, only to be told there are no timeslots left until October. If you're met with such obstinacy, however, and tell the receptionist that you are privately insured, you'll find a next-day appointment will often magically open up. That being said, if you find yourself coming down with something serious and desperately need a consultation, simply stating that you're willing to pay out of pocket will probably get you the appointment you need. Be aware that some doctors only accept private patients, so if you are publicly insured, determine by phone whether your doctor is a *Kassenarzt* (one who accepts patients from a *Gesetzliche Krankenkasse* or state health insurance provider).

If you think you can avoid the whole thing by simply avoiding health insurance, think again. The law requires that every German citizen or resident be insured continuously, from arrival to departure (or in a German's case, from birth to death). Failing to obtain health insurance can result in hefty fines that make the money you save negligible. What's more, proof of health insurance is one of the most crucial components of any visa application. Without it, you will be unable to obtain permission to work, or even to stay in Germany for very long.

There is no one-size-fits-all solution to health insurance in Germany. There are some companies, like DKV (Deutsche Krankenversicherung) that offer both public and private, but will not allow you to go with the public option until you have lived in Germany for a year or more (for proof of which you will of course need your Anmeldebestätigung). There are others, like the AXA-underwritten ALC or A La Carte healthcare, that are private, international providers who nonetheless offer relatively similar coverage to private insurers in Germany, and are therefore accepted by the German authorities. As a woman, you will need to buy an option that includes coverage for pregnancy and childbirth, whether or not you plan on having children in Germany. Otherwise, you may be turned down for a visa. Most public health plans will pay for you to get at least one general and one dental checkup per year. Private plans can be pickier, refusing to pay for anything that doesn't directly correlate to illness or injury. They are also less likely to cover prescription drugs, but you'll find most pharmaceuticals surprisingly affordable in Germany.

Your insurance policy can be a secure fallback or an irritating burden, depending on which provider you choose. If your knowledge of German is poor, assessing your options can be extremely difficult, as most policies, like most legal documents, seem designed to confuse even German natives. Consulting with an advisor can be worth your time and money, but take care that whomever you speak to is not beholden to one insurance company or another: many brokers bill themselves as advisors but are really only pushing one company's policy. Advisors are more likely to help you compare and contrast policies. With public policies, there isn't much difference in terms of price, but the value offered can vary. If your reading German is decent, the consumer rights magazine *Stiftung Warentest* does an objective comparison of healthcare plans each year.

For private options, be prepared to undergo a rigorous interview about your personal medical history, followed by a physical and dental checkup. This will determine whether you will be accepted, what type of plan you are able to get, and how much you'll have to pay. Since most full-time employees, students, and retirees choose public health insurance, which makes up about 85% of the German insurance market, this option is a lot less shrouded in mystery. Furthermore, it can be the only viable option if you make very little money (and do not want to sink a significant percentage into healthcare costs) or have a non-working spouse or children you would like to have covered (the public option allows non-working family members to be covered under your plan at no extra cost).

In comparison to the insurance requirements for working adults, student insurance is fairly easy to obtain, and students are only required to pay a minimal amount. How little is determined by which health plan you choose, and your university can help you. Be aware, however, that German universities won't allow you to enroll without adequate proof of coverage. According to the DAAD (Deutscher Akademischer Austausch-dienst), a program awarding international students fellow-ships to study in Germany, all state health insurance plans will cover students until the age of 30 or their 14th semester for the price of 80 Euros per month. After this deadline, they may continue with the same provider at a higher premium, or shop around for something new. If students are already 29 when they enroll, they only have the option to enroll in private health insurance, although private providers normally offer fairly competitive rates for students as well.

The good news is that sometimes Germany allows students, unlike working adults, to keep their home health insurance during their time here. This applies to the EU and countries that have signed the Schengen agreement with Germany. Inquire with your university before arrival in order to determine whether your home country coverage is adequate. If you are here to take a German course, you should also inquire with your language school as to what companies they would recommend. Your natural instinct may be to go for the cheapest plan, but don't assume that the cheapest plan will be adequate. Read the fine print and make a list of what is important to you. Then check to see if your plan provides it.

As with any system offering its participants two starkly different options, there is a third way. This is one of those nice little gifts that make Germany and Berlin such a great place for artists and creative people, and is no doubt one of the reasons the country has a consistently high level of culture. Freelance artists (including musicians, journalists, writers, translators, actors, and just about anyone working in the visual and performing arts) are eligible to become members of the **Künstlersozialkasse** (KSK) or artists' social security fund. This government-run agency is not an actual health insurance provider, but rather facilitates heath insurance, nursing insurance, and retirement plans for artists. If you can prove you make a large percentage of your income from your art, the government will cover half of your monthly premiums.

This program is unique in the world, started only a few decades ago as part of postwar Germany's attempt at becoming an economical and cultural powerhouse. It assumes that very few artists have full-time jobs, and that very few arts companies and organizations could afford healthcare subsidies for their workers anyway. Instead, companies that deal in arts and culture or employ a certain number of freelance creatives are asked to pay into the system just as KSK members do, thereby subsidizing the money the government puts in.

In many ways, getting into the KSK is even harder than obtaining a visa in Germany. In order to be granted KSK membership, the applicant must prove that his work is almost entirely of an artistic kind—and the criteria are strict. At its surface, the KSK accepts writers, but they usually have to be writers of books, or journalists. PR writing doesn't count, and online writing or blogging may not either. If you are a translator of literary works, you'll make it into the KSK. If most of your income is derived from translating technical manuals or publicity materials, you probably won't. Work as a chef or baker is not included (although it should be) as Germany considers this skilled labor, not art. Your application will need to include a copy of your CV translated into German, any academic credentials you may have, and even business cards and a link to your personal website. The idea is to paint a picture of yourself as an artist actually living off your work, so you'll need to provide invoices, as well as work samples corresponding to those invoices and bank statements showing that you were paid the exact amount you invoiced for.

Over the past few years, the KSK has been the subject of much speculation. A program that sounds too good to be true, many argue, usually is. As with other public insurance options, it seems inevitable that rising healthcare costs will make it impossible to keep the KSK as it is now. It is difficult to police the private companies that are required to put money into the system, and to make sure KSK members, who by-and-large self-report their income and type of work, are being as honest as possible about how "artistic" their work is. Then there is also the question about the value of the arts in general, and whether this is something the government should be funding at all. For the moment, Germany's answer is still yes.

In theory, citizens of countries that are part of the European Economic Area (EEA), including the EU, Iceland, Norway, and Lichtenstein, can use a **European Health Insurance Card** (EHIC) to prove coverage within the EU system, which enables them to receive treatment in a foreign country while still enrolled in their health plan back home. While this is an excellent option for EU citizens who don't want to deal with the hassle of deciphering the German healthcare system, it also comes with some limitations: some treatments may not be covered by your home country's health insurance, some only partially. In addition, be aware that in many non-emergency cases, you will be asked to provide payment up front, claiming a refund later using your EHIC.

All of this is only valid, however, if your stay in Germany is temporary (as a student, for example, or to work abroad for a couple of years). If you plan on making a home here for good, it makes the most sense—and indeed is only legal—to declare yourself an official resident and take on both the burdens and rewards of German health insurance. This may not seem like a good investment in your youth, but can end up paying off in the end, as the German state—and therefore German healthcare providers—tends to put a lot of stock in caring for the elderly. This in turn is why Germany's aging population and low birth rates have proven so problematic in recent years, with more and more elderly people collecting the money they invested into the social system (not just healthcare) over their lifetimes and not enough young, healthy, working people to make up the difference. This may lead to sweeping changes in the next few years, but in the midst of the political hubbub, it is worth noting that Germany is immensely proud of its healthcare system, and it works immensely well.

OTHER TYPES OF INSURANCE
AND WHETHER YOU REALLY NEED THEM

Germans really like their insurance, so much so that often-times, a type of insurance that doesn't even exist in your home country is something a German would shudder to think about living without. The so-called *Haftpflichtversicherung* or liability insurance is chief among these—at its heart, a type of insurance for any harm you might get up to once you've left your own home. If you're on your bike and collide with a pedestrian, this insurance will pay damages. If you're at a friend's house and happen to break a priceless antique, this insurance will provide the money to replace the item. Even in a dispute with a landlord over potential harm done to his property, *Haftpflicht* can help. Whereas in many Western countries someone hit by a moving target might sue, no one does that in Germany. Instead, they all have *Haftpflichtversicherung*. If this all sounds a bit absurd to you, it sounds completely and entirely crucial to Germans. Mention that you don't have it, and you may be met with audible gasps as the Germans around you move away, worried they'll catch your disease. Unfortunately, the fact that everyone in Germany has it means the society is built around the concept; as with many other societal rules, you don't want to be caught not following this one. *Haftpflichtversicherung* will only cost you around 35-60 Euros per year, however, and you can buy it from just about any bank where you have an account, or any company offering health insurance.

Hausratversicherung (household effects insurance) is also quite popular in Germany, insuring the contents of a household against theft, fire, water damage, and more. Not to be confused with homeowner's insurance, this is yet another type of insurance Germans often buy for peace of mind and a sense of control in the face of uncontrollable circumstances. It is entirely up to you whether to pursue it, and should be based on the worth, both financial and sentimental, of the items in your home. If you've only just moved here with the clothes on your back, you probably won't need this one.

While we're on the subject, if you are renting your apartment, joining a **Mieterverein** or renter's union can be invaluable. With offices all over the city, these small counseling organizations are about as socialist as it gets. For a nominal fee (again, around 30 Euros a year), you will have access to lawyers who can help with any issue that may arise due to your status as a tenant, anywhere from giving you legal advice in a quick session to representing you in court against your landlord. If you join a *Mieterverein*, you can go to them for help when you feel your landlord has increased your rent too much or hasn't carried out crucial repairs. You can go to them if construction noise is interfering with your quality of life, and they will help write a letter to your landlord to request a decrease in rent (believe it or not, this is actually possible here—the landlord can decrease your rent while the work is being done, and apply to the city to be paid the difference). Like *Haftpflichtversicherung*, membership in a Mieterverein may seem a bit odd until you really need it.

The **Rentenkasse** or pension plan is not really a type of insurance the way the others are, but is seen as equally crucial for those working in Germany long-term, especially those planning to stay into old age. If you have a full-time job, a percentage of your wages deducted automatically each month will go to your health insurance and pension plan. Don't worry if you don't plan on staying forever, though: if after five years you decide that living in Germany isn't for you, you can apply to have this money repaid after you've left the country. (Freelancers are not yet required to pay into a pension plan, but should still consider putting something aside for retirement.)

Rechtsschutzversicherung or legal protection insurance, covers pretty much everything else you can think of that doesn't fall into the previous categories. In general, this type of insurance will cover you for legal disputes involving contracts, problems with employers, disputes over rentals and purchased real estate, and vehicular disputes. In most cases, however, no insurance provider will allow you to sign up for *Rechtsschutz* after a dispute has begun, so give a thought to it when life is easy, and it may save you when things get tough.

APPLYING FOR A VISA

At last, we come to it. First, you may want to sit down. Then breathe. Then realize that you're in a uniquely privileged position: in spite of what you may have been told, Germany does not want to make this hard on you. In fact, it is one of the easiest places in the EU to get a visa. There are four main types of visas you can get as foreigner in Germany. They are, in descending order of difficulty, a full-time work visa, a freelance visa, a retiree or pensioner's visa, and a student visa.

We won't spend too much time on the first, for a number of reasons. First of all, a **full-time work visa** is nearly impossible to get unless a company offers you a full-time position before you get here, in effect "inviting" you to Germany. It is possible if you work for an international company that may happen to have an office here. It can happen if you are highly skilled (Germany is in such dire, continual need of workers with scientific, mathematical, or engineering degrees that it might offer to move your entire family here). It can also happen if a company has decided, for whatever reason, that you are a better fit for a certain position than any other EU candidate they were able to find (and is able to prove it). It probably won't happen if you simply arrive in Berlin and send a CV to a couple of companies. You will most likely be rejected outright, as giving the job to you over an EU citizen would create an enormous amount of paperwork for the company, as well as sending untold expenses their way.

A **freelance visa** can be easier to obtain, but even more perplexing in terms of paperwork, as everyone seems to have a different story about it, and no one on the official side of things (meaning, at the *Ausländerbehörde*) ever seems to be able to tell you exactly what they are looking for. No matter. There are a few documents that will be crucial to your application, and a few more you may want to take along for comfort, though don't be surprised if no one asks for them. In order to apply for a freelancer's visa, you will need:

- your passport, a biometric passport photo, and your *Anmeldebestätigung*
- proof of health insurance
- a translated copy of your CV

- a bank statement proving you have enough savings to last you six months of potential unemployment
- letters from at least three companies explaining why they plan on hiring you

Don't be surprised if you are made to whittle down your work expectations to the easiest, most readily comprehensible labels. Although in many countries, working freelance means working in many different fields and combining several skill sets, Germans (especially *Beamten*) can have trouble comprehending why you would want to split your time and energy among so many things. Germans put particular stock in official degrees, though, so if you've set your sights on a visa in advertising or PR, you'd better have some kind of college degree or course certificate on hand to prove you have the background for it.

The letters you obtain from potential employers should not only support whatever you declare as your profession, they should also give a thought to your background, and why the company believes you will be a good fit for them. This can be the most difficult part of the entire application process. A plus, though: the letters you turn in with your application do not have to be from the same companies that eventually hire you. Don't worry if you did a one-off gig for a company and want them to write you a letter, but are unsure if they'll hire you again. If they don't, it won't matter; the most important thing you'll get from them is that crucial letter.

Your CV should of course also be in German, and should demonstrate some background in the field you hope to enter. Do not simply translate word for word—the German CV or *Lebenslauf* (discussed in Chapter 9) has a certain design to it. Finally, the bank statement: there is no steadfast rule about how much money you should have in your account, but do a quick calculation of your basic costs and ask yourself the same question they will ask you. Freelancing is a tough business, even without the added pressure of a new country. The requirement that you have some money under your mattress is a safety measure for both you and Germany: they don't want you to end up on unemployment benefits and neither do you.

Obtaining legal residence in Germany as a retiree or a "person of means" used to be easier. Since the dense knot of bureaucracy around getting a visa is mostly a protection against foreigners stealing German citizens' jobs, one would think that swooping into Germany, declaring you've got a lot of money to spend and don't need to work, and demanding that you be allowed to do so forever would be a surefire way to get a visa. If you think this is too good to be true, you're not alone: so does the *Ausländerbehörde*. It is still possible to get a visa that includes a residence permit without work permission. It has become a lot more difficult to do so, however, since most *Beamten* at the *Ausländerbehörde*, unless they are incredibly gullible or far too nice, will assume you're only going to find *Schwarzarbeit* (literally "black work" or illegal work) anyway. If you're going into retirement and planning on moving to Germany, you will most certainly need proof of your pension plan translated into German, any other proof of means (bank accounts, savings, stocks and bonds) you may have, and of course, good old German health insurance.

If you come from Canada, Australia, New Zealand, Japan, South Korea, Taiwan, or Hong Kong and are between 18 and 30, you can also apply for a **12-month working holiday visa**. The idea is to give citizens of these countries insight into German culture and daily life, with the assumption that the invitation is reciprocal. Although these visas are a great way to test the waters in Germany and make valuable contacts for a potential permanent move, it is not the best idea to rely on them completely, as they can only be granted once.

Student visas, the quickest and easiest of the bunch, are available in two types: the *Studienvorbereitung* or "study preparation," and the university study visa. Visas are also available for winners of scholarships or fellowships (such as the Fulbright or the DAAD), but these are almost always connected to a university that supplies the student with research facilities and an advisor, and hence are very similar to a university visa. The *Studienvorbereitung* is perfect for you if you're just moving to Berlin to check it out for a few months, as it makes your residency permit contingent upon your attending language classes. Some schools, like the respected, world-renowned Goethe-Institut, will give you a certificate of enrollment that will be enough to get you a visa quite easily. Others, although you'll have to ask around to find out which ones, may allow you to enroll in classes for only three months while giving you a certificate for six, or for six months while giving you a certificate for twelve, giving you the option of staying in Berlin for twice as long as your classes last. Of course, in both cases, proof of student health insurance is a must.

Enrolling yourself in one of Berlin's many universities or technical colleges is also a reliable way of getting a student visa, as schools will usually take care of this automatically. If you're coming from the US or the UK, you'll find that being a student is a pretty good way to guarantee just about anything, be it a visa to stay in Germany or steep discounts on everything from concert tickets to public transit. Germany's educational system is one of the best in the world, but it can also appear extremely laid back and drawn out to those not used to it. Germans often study well into their thirties, taking breaks in between getting their degrees so that a five-year program can quickly turn into a ten-year one. Of course, you won't have the benefit of being quite so casual about it, as a gap in your studies will also correspond to a gap in your visa. For this type of visa, you will need:

- your passport, a biometric passport photo, and your *Anmeldebestätigung*
- a certificate of enrollment in a language school or university
- proof of student health insurance
- a letter from a parent or guardian avowing financial support if necessary

YOUR BIG DAY AT THE *AUSLÄNDERBEHÖRDE*

Making a visa appointment used to be more difficult, so rejoice in the fact that you live in the 21st century. Once upon a time, visa hopefuls had to line up as early as 5 in the morning at any time of year. (If you haven't spent a winter in Berlin yet, just know that 5 am is a pretty miserable time to line up in the cold). Nowadays, you can register online at www.berlin.de/labo/auslaender/dienstleistungen. Click on the link for "Terminvereinbarung" and the UK flag to switch to English. You will be taken to a page with three options: making an appointment, changing one, or canceling one. Clicking on the first will take you to a scroll-down menu where you may select your nationality. After you do so, a new scroll-down menu will appear with all the visa options available. Selecting one will give you the house, floor, and waiting room where you must appear for your appointment, along with a full list of what makes you eligible, what you will need to bring, and what the fee will be. Once you click the box to confirm that you meet the requirements, you will then be taken to a calendar where you can select open dates. Make sure you keep your confirmation email after booking, as it will have your waiting number and appointment room. Have all your papers in order the night before and be punctual. If you've heard anything about the Germans, it is that they applaud punctuality. In this case, however, being on time could save you more than embarrassment: it could be the difference between starting the process now and having to make another appointment for a month from now.

Berlin's *Ausländerbehörde* must have been designed to be as inconvenient as possible. It is located on a fairly desolate bank of the canal that goes through Wedding, with only a couple of industrial buildings to keep it company. It is accessible by both S-Bahn and U-Bahn, but a 10-15 minute walk from both. Once you arrive and enter the courtyard, you'll see several doors leading to several wings of the building, each with a letter. Choose the one that was given to you when you registered online, and find your way to the correct floor for your visa type and the correct waiting area according to the first letter of your last name. Be prepared to wait a while—this is where it can help to bring a friend for moral support, and, if you are not yet fluent, preferably a German-speaking one for language support.

Once your number appears on the display, go straight to the room number indicated, knock politely, and then go in. Greet the person you have been assigned to by name if possible (in most cases, you will be given his or her name when you register online), as it is always nice to start things off with the acknowledgment that, as mentioned earlier, you are both just people. Once you tell them what type of visa you want, they will in some cases provide you with a form requesting personal details like your name and address as well as an explanation of what you plan on doing and why your background fits it. They will then ask to see certain types of documents, including health insurance forms, letters of intent from employers, and bank statements. It can be difficult to know on any given day, based on any given person, what will satisfy the *Ausländerbehörde*, but the steadfast rule that applies in all walks of life also applies here: better be safe than sorry. Better to bring along much more than you need so that you can overwhelm them with documents if they appear to have even the slightest doubt, than to come up empty-handed. Sit quietly as they look over everything, and remember that old adage from childhood: only speak when spoken to. The last thing you want is to appear indignant over the time it takes, or as any kind of a troublemaker to the people who may decide whether you have a future in Germany.

Whether or not you walk out instantly with your visa will depend largely on what type of visa you're hoping to get. Student visas are fairly straightforward, and do not require the permission of any outside bodies. Freelance work visas, as you might imagine, are a lot more complicated, and require consent not only from the *Ausländerbehörde* but also from Berlin's *Senatsverwaltung* or city senate, who will review your application in detail while making sure there are no Germans who could ostensibly do your job. For freelancers, however, there are exceptions: if you are an artist, it is reasonably assumed that what you do artistically is unique to you; no one else could fill your shoes. If you are a journalist or an English teacher, the same rule applies: the *Ausländerbehörde* may be able to grant you your visa on the spot, provided you have your papers in order. If you are unsuccessful the first time around, don't panic: very rarely will they give you an unequivocal no and send you home. Normally, they will grant you at least a second chance, printing out an absurdly long piece of paper that will act as your temporary visa and scheduling you another appointment on the spot.

Last but not least, for any visa (except the *Studienvorbereitung*) you will need to prove some basic knowledge of German. This is easy enough, however, since as soon as you've had the meeting at the *Ausländerbehörde* and managed to squeak out who you are and what type of visa you want, they will probably deem your German acceptable. Bringing a German friend along, as suggested earlier, is not at all frowned upon, but be prepared to talk, even if you have a German with you.

OPENING A BANK ACCOUNT

If you are an EU citizen, opening a bank account can be as easy as visiting the bank with your passport and proof of residence (*Anmeldebestätigung*). If you are studying here, showing up with your student ID (even for a language class) can be enough to get you a free student account until you turn thirty. Other banks have varying requirements as to proof of employment and proof of a certain income threshold, but for non-EU citizens, one rule almost always applies: you need to be able to show some kind of residence and work or study permit. (If you had neither, there would be no legal reason for you to open a bank account here.) Where you go from there is entirely up to you, but be prepared to deal with the banks in German or bring along a German friend: a few Berlin banks may have English-speaking employees on hand, but you won't know until you go. Luckily, nowadays you also have the Internet: many banks allow you to open an account online if you're only going for the simplest option, meaning online banking and a bank card called an EC (electronic cash) or maestro card.

There are different types of banks in Germany: public, private, and somewhere in between. Private banks like Deutsche Bank operate much like private companies, and can be a lot pickier about who their customers are and a lot riskier about what they do with their money. Public banks like Sparkasse are backed by the German government, and are generally considered the best option for the man on the street, the average German citizen. In the middle are the so-called *Volksbanken* or people's banks, cooperative banks in which account holders are like members, each assuming a certain amount of liability and reaping benefits. Many banks will allow you to open free accounts as long as your monthly deposits are over a certain minimum, and several will even give you cash incentives to sign up. When choosing a bank in Berlin, do a search online to see how many bank branches turn up, as this will have a rather limiting effect on your ability to withdraw cash when you need it. Unlike many other European capitals, Berlin is an ATM wasteland: even if you sign up with a ubiquitous bank like Berliner Sparkasse, you may end up feeling like there's never a *Geldautomat* (cash machine) around when you need one.

Credit cards can be issued along with accounts at certain thresholds, but are not that necessary. For the most part, Germany is still a cash-based society, and Germans are still quite debt-averse (perhaps another reason the country has weathered the financial upheavals so well). Even if you think a Berlin establishment like a fancy restaurant or upscale shop must take credit cards, be prepared to be astonished when you pull out your Visa card and are met with a perplexed look: Germans almost always use their EC card to pay for small purchases, bank transfers or *Überweisungen* to pay for large ones, simply because it is a sensible life choice: if you only pay by bank card or directly from you bank account, you'll never spend money you don't have.

Once you've opened your bank account, it is a good idea to use it as much as possible while in Germany. Even if you still have money left in a home account, this money can be pricy to come by, as it will need to be transferred to your German bank before you can use it or withdrawn from an ATM in Germany, both of which can incur hefty currency conversion charges, as well as international withdrawal or transfer charges. High-yield savings accounts and investment options are also available at most banks, and can be particularly lucrative at the private ones. If you have a good amount of cash saved up in your home country, you might consider transferring it over to a German bank. Very often, for big investments like obtaining a mortgage to buy property in Germany, or even for renting your first Berlin apartment, potential sellers or landlords won't even consider savings you've accumulated outside of Germany. Transfer that money to your trusty German bank, and somehow it suddenly becomes valid.

FINDING A PLACE TO LIVE

Finding a home in a big city can be a daunting task, and the type of housing and neighborhood you choose can have lasting effects on your quality of life and your sense of both self and surroundings. In searching for a place to live, you'll have to dig pretty deep into your psyche, asking yourself some tough questions. Before embarking on your search, you should know how you live best, with whom you live best, how much space you need, and how much you want to spend. Then, prepare to be tested: Berlin's real estate market used to have a reputation as a piece of cake, but its waters have grown murkier in the past few years, its standards higher. Still, in comparison to most other popular cities in the world, Berlin continues to be a great deal. As long as you keep your expectations in check, you'll be able to find something you're relatively happy with for a price that's still around a fifth of what you would pay in London or Paris. What's more, the search can be fun and educational, allowing you to see how normal Berliners live while envisioning yourself in scenarios you may never have thought you'd inhabit so comfortably. If Berlin is about imagination and reinvention, finding a place to live is a perfect way to play with both.

THE REAL ESTATE MARKET TODAY: EXPECTATIONS VS. REALITY

Up until recently, when Berlin was seized with a kind of real estate mania the city had never seen before, it was still much more of a renter's market here than a buyer's. In contrast to other major European cities, becoming a property owner did not necessarily lead to a financial windfall, and sticking with renting over buying did not necessarily mean that a tenant had to fear for the future of his living space. True, now many more people want in on both sides, and those people generally have a lot more money than they used to. This, inevitably, has meant a significant rise in rents in the last half decade. The ugliest word on everyone's lips is no racial slur, it seems, but rather, "**gentrification**," and in Berlin its effects have been swift, as a city stuck in an economic quagmire for decades races to catch up. For many of Berlin's oldest and poorest citizens, it isn't that rents are rising with such ferocity, but rather that Berlin salaries have not kept pace with the cost of living.

Someone with expertise in economics might demand to know how this is possible. Well, there's been a lot of debate about that, and a lot of false assumptions. Some Berliners contend that foreigners are the problem—all the expats (people like you!) coming to newly hip areas like Neukölln and Kreuzberg are accepting rents no local would tolerate, driving landlords to raise them even higher. Well, yes and no. The fact is, gentrification in Berlin officially started the moment the Wall fell, but most of the so-called "foreigners" colonizing Berlin's new neighborhoods in the East were actually...Germans! (But West Germans, and therefore equally as foreign to East Berliners as someone coming from across an ocean.) A lot of fingers have also been pointed at tourists, but they rarely stay long enough to become part of the problem: a weeklong visitor certainly won't be competing with you to sign a lease.

There is something to be said, however, for another trade fueled by tourism: that of short-term rentals, or so-called **holiday apartments**. Aided by websites like Airbnb, which allow anyone to rent out any type of property online, some Berlin residents now make a living off renting out multiple apartments to tourists for short-term stays. Many have been going one step further: buying apartments just to rent them out as so-called *Ferienwohnungen* or holiday rentals instead of as real homes to steady tenants. This practice effectively takes a significant number of potential rentals off the market, narrowing the pickings for people who actually live here. It has been acknowledged as a real problem in the media, enough so that Berliners (and of course hotels, who are losing crucial revenue) are calling on politicians to set new laws about who can rent out apartments. The newspaper *Spiegel International* has already reported that politicians are planning to set much more stringent regulations in Berlin over short-term rentals, but it is still unclear whether this will lead to a crackdown, or indeed if these new rules will be enforceable at all.

Yet another problem is Berlin's **growing population**. The city is no longer a secret anymore, and people seem to be moving here by the truckload, many of them with more money than the average Berliner and already used to higher living costs. To these newcomers, whether a *Beamter* coming from Germany's southwest to take a new government job or a Brit still propped up by a substantial London salary, paying 1000 Euros a month or more for an apartment is a steal. To those who have lived here for decades, it looks like highway robbery. Berlin's comparatively low housing prices are also a reason why so many real estate vultures have descended upon the city en masse. Nowadays, it isn't too unusual to see entire blocks of flats bought up by one person or company, only to be cleared of their tenants, renovated lavishly, and sold off at three times the price. Just as with Berlin's streets and public squares, Berlin's buildings are being covered in scaffolding and laid into by jackhammers, only to emerge clean and shiny a year later. Again, certain neighborhoods have begun to fight back, with Pankow leading the way as the first district to prohibit new luxury renovations.

Finally, recent **deregulation** has only exacerbated the problem, causing steep rent hikes in some former working class neighborhoods. The word "deregulation," though, can mean a couple of things: first of all, landlords who received government money to renovate their properties soon after the Wall fell were obliged to offer these apartments at very low rates for a certain period of time. Many of those obligations are now expiring, freeing landlords who have long suffered under them, making laughably small amounts of rental income since 1989, to charge market rate at last. Another form of deregulation is the selling of large numbers of government-owned and therefore government-regulated units to private owners who are then free to raise rents, forcing a lot of poorer families to leave areas where they may have put down roots, which in turn frees up even more rental units to be flipped. Kottbusser Tor in Kreuzberg has been the scene of several high-profile cases recently, leading to rallies and protests on behalf of the families getting kicked out.

Even now, it's hard to say what will happen in the next few years. Prices are still rising, people are still coming, and happily, some new housing is being built (though mostly on the higher end of the real estate market). Is Berlin doomed to become the next New York in terms of prices, or even the next Munich? A lot of economic factors may keep it from going down that road that quickly, not least of which is the continued lack of industry and high unemployment in the city. But who knows? If enough people with money keep coming to Berlin to buy and rent property, the city's original inhabitants may have a real problem. The oldest may have to move out of town. The youngest may simply move on to the next big thing. Poland, anyone?

WHAT'S YOUR TYPE?
BERLINERS AND HOW THEY LIVE

Despite the recent upswing in real estate sales, Berlin is still very much a renter's market. That doesn't mean Berliners are transient, though. In contrast, many of them stay in rental apartments for much of their lives. Some even do crucial renovation work on their own, making a rental apartment as much a home as their own property would be. To some, this might seem like insanity—or a surefire path to financial ruin. To Berliners, however, it is entirely reasonable, as they are improving their apartments without increasing rents (landlords are only allowed to demand sizable rent increases if they renovate apartments themselves, adding a balcony, for example, or updating the heating system). In your first few years, however, you don't necessarily have to think about settling down. Berliners tend to move around often before they find their true home…or get tired of looking.

Highly prevalent in Berlin is the so-called *Wohngemeinschaft* (WG) or "living community," a type of shared living that can be a lot more than what it sounds like. Whereas in

other countries, roommates are simply something to be toler-
ated, and a shared home merely one step on the road towards
true adulthood, Germans see the WG as more of a lifestyle
choice, something you do because you want to, regardless of
age and socio-economic status. True, a couple of students
looking to save money on housing costs might choose to share
a flat simply out of convenience, but most WGs are more than
that, uniting people with shared interests, giving each roommate instant friends and an automatic social life. Most people
who found a WG (and a WG is always "founded" or *gegrün-
det*, never simply "started") probably have a list of guidelines
in mind, which will automatically attract some potential roommates to the concept while repelling others. Is the WG veg-
etarian? Is it only for students or young professionals? Is it a
party WG or a quiet WG? Will there be weekly dinners cooked
by one member on a rotating basis? A WG founded exclusively
for the sake of saving money is often referred to as a *Zweck-
WG*. Any other will probably expect some form of socializing
among its members.

WG living has become such an ingrained part of German
society that you may encounter people living in WGs who, in
any other country, might appear to have outgrown them. It is
not uncommon for one WG member to be nearing middle
age; perhaps someone who was lucky enough to nab a large
flat around the time the Wall fell. Rather than find a new place
after meeting, many couples live quite happily with roommates. Even single mothers with young children (so-called
Alleinerziehende) pop up now and then in an online search
of WGs. WG members can get so used to the easy relationship they have with their roommates and the natural family
they create, it can be tough to leave it all behind. Perhaps this
is why WG living is not merely the domain of the young and
penniless, and not only considered a temporary, inferior form
of living, but rather open to all and enjoyed by many.

As one might expect from the diversity and abundance
of WGs in Berlin, it is really the only viable student option.
Elsewhere, starting university also means moving into large
student dormitories that act as a sort of quasi-independent
bridge into adult life. But with Berlin WGs, most students are
thrown directly into adulthood. They have to negotiate the

signing of a lease, contract with an electricity company, buy furniture, paint and decorate, and make sure roommates do their fair share of housework, all immediately after leaving the family home. True, some university fellowship programs, such as the Fulbright, will offer their fellows placement with a local family. Some German schools, like the Goethe-Institut, will also offer enrolled students the use of housing placement services. Other international student programs will offer limited student housing in buildings near campus that are the closest thing you'll get to "dorms" (see Chapter 8). But for the most part, these options are expensive, can be isolating, and pale in comparison to the experience you'll gain from living in a WG.

In contrast to the almighty WG, of course, living alone or with a partner or spouse can seem positively square. In applying for a place alone or as a couple, you will often find yourself at an advantage, though: a lot of landlords won't even consider WGs, which have a reputation, whether true or purely fabricated, for being loud party houses full of inconsiderate youngsters. In contrast, approach a landlord with plans to set up your own quiet domicile, or as a starry-eyed couple who may eventually start a family, and you are more likely to be given a warm welcome.

Keep in mind however, that even **living alone** isn't really living alone in Berlin. Berliners are a tight-knit bunch, and at some point everyone has either had a complaint about a so-called "*Stasi* neighbor"—named after the East German secret police who would monitor every aspect of GDR citizens' lives—or been one. But there can be advantages to living in a building where, to put it bluntly, everyone knows your name. Even if you're a young single, new to the city and living alone in a studio apartment, befriending the old woman two floors up may lead to a wealth of stories, or at the very least, someone who will accept your deliveries. If there's a rowdy WG directly underneath you, consider being polite instead of turning up your nose—you might just need one of them to help you haul a sofa upstairs. Many buildings in Berlin, especially those with long-term tenants, can also act as ersatz-WGs, scheduling *Hof* (courtyard) grill parties for the entire apartment house in warm weather or planning a *Weihnachtsplätzchen*

(Christmas cookie) baking session for all the tenants' children in the kitchen of the building's proverbial grandma. Indeed, you may sometimes forget you live in a city for how well you get to know the people around you. Sure, most cities can be anonymous, with all the advantages and disadvantages that may entail, but then, most cities are not Berlin.

FINDING A FLAT: DOS AND DON'TS

Now that you've read a bit about how difficult yet rewarding it can be to find a place in Berlin, it's time to begin your own personal treasure hunt. The only problem is, the map is in a different language, and there's no "X marks the spot."

Whatever you do, don't go the easy route of **Craigslist**. Americans may know it as the first and indeed only website for finding property. Most Germans, however, have never heard of it, and that means hardly any locals ever go there to search for what they need. Unfortunately, the people who post on Craigslist know that their audience is made up of a bunch of enthusiastic, overly trustworthy new expats who don't speak German. (If they did, they would be on one of many German websites looking for apartments.) Instead, new Berliners who end up on Craigslist will find themselves sifting through ads for holiday rentals on Mallorca and too-good-to-be-true luxury apartments with accompanying photos that look unlike any type of building in Berlin. There are many scams here, and for a reason: people only resort to using Berlin Craigslist when they have nowhere else to turn. That means they're probably desperate, and that makes them far more likely to fork over a large sum of money for an apartment that doesn't exist.

Instead of falling down the Craigslist rabbit hole, take a look at a number of dependable housing websites, all of which have sections just for Berlin. Named after **Immobilien**, the German word for real estate, literally an "unmoveable" or "immobile" piece of property, sites like Immobilienscout or Immowelt are used mostly by real estate agents (called *Makler* in German), who post listings for which they expect to receive a finder's fee or *Provision*. These websites are the most comprehensive, offering dozens of new listings in every neighborhood, at every price point, every day. Of course, because they are so popular, everyone else is using them too. This can put you at a disadvantage, or at least at the mercy of sheer dumb luck, especially when you're one of a hundred people trying to contact an agent about a particularly attractive listing. Many Berliners choose to forego this route, instead using peer-to-peer websites like WG-gesucht or Studenten-WG. Here, established WGs with an empty room to fill and those looking to found new WGs post ads for roommates. People moving out of rentals also look for what's called a *Nachmieter*, someone who takes over the remainder of the lease and, with any luck, signs the next contract as *Mieter* (renter and leaseholder). Although these websites are almost as highly frequented as Immobilienscout, they offer better deals, as old tenants may be able to recommend you directly to their *Vermieter* (landlord) or *Hausverwaltung* (property management), allowing you to jump the line and avoid pricy agent fees.

Of course, the ability to navigate these handy and helpful websites is still contingent upon one thing: a vague grasp of German housing vocabulary. Don't worry, though. You don't need to be able to read Goethe in order to decipher a simple apartment listing. The two most important terms you need to know are *Kalt-* and *Warmmiete*, which translate directly into "cold" and "warm" rent. On any given website, you will be searching by one or the other. The **Kaltmiete** is the rental price without any extras, while **Warmmiete** is traditionally the Kaltmiete with so-called Nebenkosten or extras, fees the landlord must pay for the monthly upkeep of the apartment, such as trash collection and cleaning of common spaces. Sometimes the *Warmmiete* includes heating, but be careful about this: a building can have several different types of heating. Some of them, like **Fernwärme** or "distance heating," are supplied to the entire building from a power plant that can be far away (hence the name), with costs divided among tenants according to living space. In buildings with gas heating, however, there is one unit per apartment or floor, called **Gasetagenheizung**, and each living space is charged according to use. Be aware that *Warmmiete* is sort of a misnomer: it is the highest price you will have to pay your landlord, but not necessarily an all-inclusive sum, as you will also have to contract sepa-

rately with companies for your electricity and phone. Expect a bill from your landlord at the end of the year with extra, unforeseen costs—the *Nebenkosten* are based on previous years' costs of upkeep, but it is hard to calculate these exactly. Be on the lookout for those end-of-year bills that seem too high: landlords who cannot legally raise the rent may try to get in a few extra hundred Euros by scattering "fake" costs throughout bills they don't expect their tenants to study too closely.

In addition, look for further keywords and catchphrases to describe what you'll be getting. An **Altbau**, as detailed earlier, will probably be a pre-1940s building with high ceilings (*hohe Decken*), wooden floors (*Holzdielen* or *Parkett*) and sometimes fancy moldings at the ceiling (*Stuck*). Every once in a

^ *Old buildings, cafés, and streetlife along Kreuzberg's popular Bergmannstraße*

while, you will get some particularly well-preserved old flats that might feature a ceramic tile oven (*Kachelofen*), and very often you'll see places advertised with a bay window (*Erker*), a balcony (*Balkon*), or a terrace (*Terrasse*). Most of them have the traditional Berlin set up of a front house (*Vorderhaus*), one or two side wings (*Seitenflügel*) and sometimes, but not always, a back house (*Hinterhaus* or *Gartenhaus*) surrounding a courtyard. Most of these buildings only have five floors, starting with the ground floor or *Erdgeschoss* and capped with a penthouse or *Dachgeschoss*, either a conversion of an old attic level or a completely new unit added onto the roof. Apartments can get increasingly expensive as floors get higher, since higher floors mean more sunlight (something Berliners crave above all else, although perplexingly, they also pine after tree-lined streets, even though large trees block sunlight). If you're lucky enough to nab one of those coveted top-level flats, though, prepare for some fitness training: most *Altbau* buildings have no elevator (*Fahrstuhl*). You may also come across many listings that boast of a **Berliner Zimmer**. These rooms are uncommonly large and can sometimes have a comically elongated shape, as they traditionally served as the connecting space between *Vorderhaus* and *Seitenflügel* back when each floor was an entire apartment. While real estate agents seem to treasure the Berliner Zimmer, in fact they are all courtyard-facing rooms by default. Most only have one window and are hence quite dark. *Altbau* apartments in the *Vorderhaus* or *Seitenflügel* will likely have one of them: just don't fall into the trap of thinking they're anything special.

The designation of **Neubau** is given to anything built after the war, so the term can be a bit of a grab bag. A *Neubau* in Friedrichshain, for example, could mean one of the impressive and highly coveted *Stalinbau* buildings lining Karl-Marx-Allee. It could also mean a newly constructed townhouse in the district of Rummelsburg. In old West Berlin, it usually means a boxy, low-ceilinged, unattractive building with tiny windows and imitation wood (*Laminat*) or PVC floors. In districts like Lichtenberg or Marzahn, it can mean stark high rises. In areas of Mitte, however, luxury *Neubau* buildings are going up a mile a minute; chic glass-and-steel complexes built by celebrity "starchitects" with price tags to match. These places may seem excessive, but some can be better deals in the long run, as they are built to the highest energy standards, saving their occupants a fortune on heating.

Sometimes you will come across an apartment described as a *Maisonettewohnung* (taken from the French word for house, *maison*), which stretches over two floors. These may seem luxurious, but check the amount of square feet and the layout: sometimes they can be quite inconvenient, with a bathroom on only one floor or a particularly small winding staircase. On sites like Immobilienscout, you may see apartments labeled "EBK" for *Einbauküche*: this means that some or all kitchen appliances are already installed—not a given in Germany. On sites like WG-gesucht or on any handover that involves a new tenant taking over from an old one, there may already be a kitchen installed, but sometimes you'll be asked to contribute payment for it, picking up some of the costs of the last renter. This is known as an *Abstand*, and although not technically legal (you cannot force someone to take over your stuff in order to take over your apartment), it is considered quite normal in Berlin.

Of course, as with many things in Berlin, the best way to go can still be word of mouth. Everyone knows someone who is moving. But be quick on your feet and quick to your phone, because places in this town go fast, and everyone—be it a tenant or a landlord—is looking to find the next tenant before the apartment is vacant for even a day. The same goes for WG members, who would much rather find a new roommate before the current one has moved out than risk a room standing empty, which they will be expected to pay for. Many WGs will have "casting calls" to fill a room, where they invite all interested potential roommates to come over at the same time. This solves the problem of conflicting schedules among current roommates, but makes the job of a potential applicant all the more difficult, as he or she must really shine in a crowd. If you're recommended by a friend, however, you can relax: with any luck these people already know you and have some idea of whether or not they want to live with you.

What should you expect on a *Wohnungsbesichtigung* or apartment viewing? Well, for starters, don't expect to be the only one there, especially in popular neighborhoods like Kreuzberg and Neukölln. Viewings all over central Berlin have become notorious for drawing crowds, sometimes to the point where you'll feel you have to elbow your way in just to get a glimpse of a hallway. On the bright side, if you're wandering an unknown street, trying to figure out where you're supposed to be, the crowd gathering outside a building is usually a good tip-off. Because of the high demand for apartments these days, expect to have to do some impressing. Dress sharp, be focused, and make sure you introduce yourself to the real estate agent, who will be the one to sort through the applications and present the best to the landlord. (Landlords rarely, if ever, show up at viewings even if they live in Berlin.) If at all possible, come armed with the full application to hand over to the agent, printed and organized in a folder. Many potential applicants show up to view an apartment completely unprepared, then frantically throw together the relevant documents and send them off as an email attachment later. If you have everything at the viewing, thereby saving the agent time and paper, you'll really set yourself apart.

What needs to be in that folder? Proof of income, called the *Einkommensnachweis*, a credit score called a **Schufaauskunft**, obtainable from a credit report agency (Easy Credit Bank at Alexanderplatz is the fastest), and proof from your previous landlord that you paid your rent on time, called the **Mietschuldenfreiheit** (certificate of release from rental debt). Agents will also give you a questionnaire or *Fragebogen* at the viewing, which almost always asks for the same things: your contact info, income, employer, reason for moving, and very often the apartment size and price you're looking for, so that the real estate agent can refer back to this if other apartments fitting your criteria come up. Make no mistake about it though: in Berlin, realtors are working for landlords, not potential tenants. (Unfairly, tenants are the ones who end up paying them by paying the *Provision*, but there's talk of new legislation to change this). Even if a real estate agent asks what you're looking for and promises to keep you in mind for other apartments, he or she most likely won't. Don't bother to put your trust in just one: an agent's job in this city is to fill vacancies for the landlord, not to help you in your apartment search.

If you have a full-time job, all you should need as proof of income is a copy of your contract and last few pay stubs. If you're a freelancer, expect to be heavily scrutinized, with much more demanded of you as proof of income than just a couple of contracts or invoices. Also expect the agent you're dealing with to act as if he's never dealt with freelancers in his life before—you'll most likely need to label and explain each piece of paper you include in your application. Some Germans have parents back them up with the inclusion of what's called an *Elternbürgschaft* or parental guarantee. For a non-German student with no steady income, however, a WG or a sublet is probably your best bet, as few landlords will accept such a guarantee from parents living abroad. This is where student placement agencies come in: you may not have your pick of the best, but you will have access to some spaces specifically set aside for students. *Studentenwerk* is a good online portal for student apartments.

Once you've been accepted, you'll be expected to sign the contract (*Mietvertrag*) and fork over a deposit, called a *Kaution*. Moving days are traditionally the 1st or 15th of the month, and most landlords will want you to start paying on one or the other, regardless of whether you can move that quickly. Of course, most landlords demand a three-month *Kündigungszeit* or cancellation time on your current lease, making it all the more crucial to find a *Nachmieter* who can take over an unfinished lease when you move out. In a way, the whole thing doesn't make much sense, but remember, once you're in an apartment, you're potentielly in for life, so it seems only expected (if not entirely fair) that landlords make the application process as hard on you as possible.

One last note about the contract: due to rapidly rising rents in Berlin and the explosive interest in the rental market here, many landlords now choose to include a provision in their contracts for **Staffelmiete** (graduated rent) making them legally within their rights to increase the rent by a fixed sum every year. This helps them, as they are no longer saddled with annoying tenants who stay on for decades without paying higher rents. But it does absolutely no service to you. There may be no way of getting around the *Staffelmiete* clause if this is an apartment you truly want, but make sure you do the math so you know what you'll be paying if you do end up staying long-term.

BUYING A HOME

Buying property in Berlin has become a lot more popular lately. Or at least, talking about buying property has. Now that rents have gotten high enough, sustaining a mortgage costs about the same as paying a landlord every month. So more people are now on the hunt, leading to a situation where everyone is talking about buying, but not so many average, middle class people actually are buying. There are a few reasons for this. As stated earlier, Berlin still remains a renter's market, and Germans in general are a lot more into renting than buying. When a lot of people live in rentals versus owned property, fewer properties come onto the market to buy, and a higher percentage of them already have tenants with old rental contracts who will be all but impossible to kick out. Who wants to spend several hundred thousand on an apartment that only yields a couple of hundred a month in rent? In most cases, potential buyers are permitted to avail themselves of the so-called "7-year limit," a law stating that if they can prove they need the property for their personal use, the current tenants have to leave in seven years. But this is harder than it sounds, and who wants to wait seven years anyway? A common move for many foreign buyers, also leading to the latest squeeze on rental properties, is to make a purchase as a *Kapitalanlage* or capital investment. In other words, buying an apartment just to sit on it (potentially even leaving it empty) until its value goes up. This is a risky proposition in the first place (When will the value go up? By how much?), but it is also fundamentally unfair. Real estate may be a very good investment, but an apartment isn't a piece of art, and Berlin is not a gigantic bank.

If you decide that buying is for you, your first step should be talking to a bank about a **Kredit** or mortgage. Ideally, you should already have an account with a bank in Germany, and this should be the first one you talk to about borrowing money. You should be able to demonstrate solid regular income—walk into a bank as a freelancer and you will most certainly be turned down, walk in as a foreigner with no funds in Germany and you probably won't get far. Banks in Germany are extremely cautious (one reason they have survived the crisis so well). If you are turned down for a mortgage in Germany, you're probably out of luck: no upstanding bank in the world will grant you a mortgage for a property in a foreign country, as they will have no control over that property if they need to repossess it.

Another option if you have capital but cannot get a loan is to go the increasingly popular route of the *Zwangsversteigerung*: court auctions on properties that have been seized because the owners could not pay their mortgages, or for other legal reasons. There are several websites that advertise properties such as these, usually at prices far beneath what they would be on the normal real estate market. There are extremely good deals to be found here, but beware: as with many things that seem too good to be true, this one also comes with a lot of caveats. The information you get before the auction date is minimal, these properties are almost always rented out, and it can be very difficult to see them in person. People are living in them, and there are no real estate agents acting as go-betweens. Most importantly, although the price listed may seem amazingly cheap, this is only the bottom line estimate the court assigns to each property; the "first bid," so to speak. A lot of interested parties will certainly bid the price up.

If you choose to go the normal buying route, however, expect it to start much like a search for a rental. One thing you'll find different, however: real estate agents tend to chase you when you're looking to buy, instead of the other way around. Of course they are always unfailingly polite: once they've made the sale they will earn a 7% **courtage** or commission. And for a property costing around 200,000 Euros or more, this can be significant. Your best bet? Engage with these people, tell them what you want, and try to make them work for you. Usually, as with rentals, they are more interested in selling properties than building relationships with potential buyers, but you may get lucky and find a good one who actually wants to help you.

Once you've found a property, your agent will relay your offer to the owner. Whereas in other countries it is expected that offers will come in under the **asking price**, it is very unusual for potential buyers in Germany to underbid, unless something is seriously wrong with the property. Still, you can always try to talk the seller down. The worst that can happen is that he or she will say no and you'll be back to the original asking price. If your offer is accepted, expect to pay additional costs adding up to 10-15% more than the property price. Aside from the courtage, you will need to factor in what's called a **Grunder-werbssteuer** (the real estate transfer tax), a *Grundbucheintrag* (a fee for having your name entered into the official property log), and the *Notarkosten* (the costs of a notary, who prepares the contract and conducts the official "signing ceremony" at the closure). Of course, even though it is not a normal part of this process, it is still advisable to hire a lawyer to look over the contract and an architect or construction specialist to go through the house with you before you make an offer. The seller is obligated to disclose any and all flaws that might not be readily apparent, along with what's called the *Eigentü-merversammlung* (minutes of the property owners' meetings, which will reveal whether or not the building is structurally sound, and if there are any major renovation projects planned, which new owners will also be obligated to contribute to). The seller is not, however, required to inform you of any obvious defects to the property; you're expected to be observant enough to figure them out yourself, and another pair of eyes—especially those of an expert—can't hurt.

In general, whether you end up renting or buying, it helps to remember that your decision is not a completely binding one. Take your time to find the right place, but don't take too long: you may find yourself rejecting several places and later regretting passing them over. Furthermore, the most important thing is to find a neighborhood and a lifestyle that make you feel comfortable, as you'll be spending a large amount of time in your home and the few blocks' radius around it. If you've found an apartment where you're happy to spend an entire winter, that's half the battle. If you're lucky enough to find it in a neighborhood that beckons you outdoors and greets you warmly once you're there, then that's the other half. If you've found both of those things for a price that suits you, then you haven't just survived the battle…you've won the war.

LEARNING GERMAN

JUST DO IT!

Berlin right now seems particularly prone to hand wringing over the issue of language, whether you've learned it, and what it says about your "right" to be here. Perhaps because it seems to be the city of the moment, lots of people are moving here without thinking it through, ostensibly forgetting that Berlin is still the capital of Germany. Discussions about the perceived reluctance of Berlin's international community to learn German generally fall into two categories: there are those who think you shouldn't have to learn any language if you don't want to and can get by without it, and those who think it should be learned as a courtesy to the locals. Of those who have been in Berlin for long enough that their lack of German seems a bit ridiculous, there are also two basic categories: some didn't learn it because it was too difficult, others because it was just too "ugly."

Then, of course, although they'd be loath to admit it, there are those who probably could learn it if they applied the effort, but have already arranged their lives well enough without it. Most Germans who speak English with their international friends are probably just trying to get in a bit of practice, but they may not realize they're doing those friends a disservice by reinforcing the notion that living in Germany without German is just fine. Perhaps it is, and perhaps you can get away with it for a few years, but if you plan on staying in Berlin long-term, and long for the feeling that you've truly integrated, there's no better way to start than by learning the language. Even if it doesn't end up being your golden ticket into the hidden, magical world you'd dreamed of, at least it'll let you order a meal in a restaurant or make an appointment at the doctor's office without embarrassing yourself.

WHAT TO EXPECT WHEN YOU'RE LEARNING GERMAN

If you've heard that German isn't the easiest of languages, you're not wrong. But it also isn't the hardest, and once you've got the basics down, it has a certain logic to it that will carry you through thick and thin. If you've learned any of the other Western European languages (French, Italian, Spanish) that are a grade school's bread and butter, they'll help little in their form and structure now. They will, however, allow you to anticipate the comical and sometimes condescending nature of learning a language as an adult: If you remember having to prance around in silly hats and write nonsensical sketches for your high school French class, learning German as a full-fledged adult will be much the same. If you can accept the fact that you'll sound like a five-year-old for at least the first couple of years, and that the hat-wearing, high-kicking antics of it all can be rather joyous, then you're well prepared to begin your first day of German language training.

If you know anything about German, it's probably that the language sounds too harsh and contains words that are far too long. In fact, on the first day of intermediate classes in some language schools, after students have learned enough to decipher a basic text but still cannot really speak, teachers who think they are being clever pass out the German translation of the famous Mark Twain essay, "The Awful German Language." With the wry spirit and great humor that were trademarks of the beloved American writer, this essay does a lot of haranguing over German's endless rules and exceptions, its nonsensical articles, and its absolutely disastrous propensity to split verbs in half. Of course, the well-meaning German teacher thinks this essay will only serve to prove to his new students that they are not alone; that the burden they are about to shoulder has already weighed down the likes of Mr. Twain and many other great masters of language. In reality, the essay is utterly terrifying. The fact that it's been translated into German (in a kind of subversion of the space-time continuum, one might think) certainly doesn't help.

The truth? The German language is tough, but you've already made the best step towards learning it by moving to Germany. In fact, if you're diligent, you can probably count on about a year of German classes before you're ready to go off on your own and learn by living. If you have a German room-mates or partner, the journey will still be an uphill climb, but the gradient won't be quite as steep. This is because, as with any new language, you'll learn it best by forcing yourself to speak it all the time, even when you might not need to. Of course, this isn't so easy in a city where most people speak some English and are so eager to practice. It also isn't particu-larly convenient when you're trying to set up your life in a new city and just want to make friends, not humiliating faux pas or, in German, *Fehltritte*. But Germans can also be remarkably understanding. Explain to them how important it is for you to practice. They'll be surprised and somewhat flattered once you demonstrate the lengths you'll go to in order to learn their "awful German language." Because the truth is, most Ger-mans are quite aware that their words are too long, their ar-ticles nonsensical, and their propensity to split verbs absolutely infuriating to the rest of us. Demonstrate that you're willing to love their language in spite of its flaws, and you'll likely find yourself earning valuable respect, which will in turn build your enthusiasm and fuel your quest to learn more.

GERMAN SCHOOLS AND THEIR RELATIVE MERITS

It is hard to think of a skill—such as learning a language in the country where it is spoken—for which the age group, edu-cational background, prior skills, and socio-economic status of those learning it could be less equal, or less relevant. Your first German class will bring you and your peers together in your utter lack of understanding, regardless of where you all come from. That being said, the strength of a school is in its ability to take each group of perplexed, somewhat panicked non-German speakers and unite them in pursuit of a common goal. Since learning a new language must involve interaction in that language, classes work best when students like each other and want to help each other instead of competing.

One school that recognizes this and does it extremely well, earning its worldwide reputation as a respected center of German language instruction, is the **Goethe-Institut**. Teachers there understand that a language has to be taught as an all-encompassing life experience, rather than just rote memorization and verb declination. Sign up for a Goethe class and you will also have access to their learning center and library, as well as a seemingly endless list of tours, events, and social activities. Classes have a reputation for being lively, engaging, and intensive, and Goethe uses its own print materials. From all this, however, it's easy to guess that Goethe is a bit pricey. In fact, it's the most expensive option in town: an eight-week intensive course can cost two thousand Euros or more, depending on the season.

At the other end of the spectrum are the *Volkshochschulen* or "people's education centers." The most economical way of learning German, these schools can be found in every Berlin neighborhood, with the declared mission of integrating the local immigrant population. Courses are dirt cheap (100 teaching hours cost 150 Euros or less) and can be hit or miss, depending on the teacher, the other students, and the centers themselves. Still, in contrast to luxury learning centers like the Goethe-Institut, where the expense means that most students are sponsored by their university or company, the experience at a *Volkshochschule* can be a real eye-opener. In fact, it may be your only chance to learn alongside people who have moved to Berlin for markedly different reasons than you: people who desperately need work to support large families, or even refugees. Unfortunately, as prices often directly correlate to quality, the Volkshochschulen are not terribly intensive: expect to encounter classes with a large number of pupils, little personal attention, and low accountability. Students routinely skip class and neglect homework as no one really bothers to check, and that means you'll really only get out of a *Volkshochschule* what you put into it. Be prepared to make the effort and do extra work on the side, but don't expect a pat on the back for it. These schools are more for those who need to learn German than for those who want to.

In between the very top and the very bottom lies a dizzying array of options. New language schools seem to open every day, but a few tried-and-true options have been around for a while, and there are reasons for that:

- The **Prolog Sprachschule** in Schöneberg offers a month of standard German classes at 20 hours per week for the price of 500 Euros. The only classes with set start dates are beginners' classes; anyone else can enroll at any time and join a class already in progress. Prolog employs two alternating teachers per class so students benefit from two teaching styles and the watchful eye of two different people. If a student is faltering or having trouble on a certain lesson plan, a change in teacher can help.
- **GLS** in Prenzlauer Berg offers a month of standard German classes at 20 hours per week for 550 Euros. Like Prolog, it allows new students to begin classes every Monday. It also offers something else that can prove invaluable: the chance for its students to practice their language skills firsthand with an internship placement.
- **Sprachsalon** in Neukölln seems more like a cozy club for expats than a language school. It offers month-long intensive courses for only 270 Euros. Sprachsalon also has a great learning-by-doing method: German language "workshops" for instruction in handy life skills like bike repair or even knitting, allowing you to learn new vocabulary almost without trying.
- **Speakeasy Sprachzeug** in Friedrichshain offers a one-month intensive German course at 12 hours a week for 280 Euros. Also offering translation and proofreading, this place is sort of a catchall for German services catering to those who get bored easily. It has everything from German language bike tours to exhibitions and events.

PRIVATE TUTORS AND TANDEM PARTNERS

Most language schools offer the opportunity to spend time with what's called a **tandem partner**—someone who speaks the language you're trying to learn and wants to learn the language you already speak—but the results can be like something out of a slapstick comedy unless you at least know how to conjugate a couple of verbs. Once you've gotten to B level with your language skills, you may be ready and excited to try them out on someone. Ask your school to direct you to their pinboard listings for tandem partners or go straight to the Internet: The language and tutoring portal **Erste Nachhilfe** always has extensive listings for Germans looking to practice with native speakers. The search portal **Sprachduo** allows you to enter in your city and the language you wish to learn, and then see who comes up. Once you find a tandem partner, just as with a blind date, arrange to meet him or her in a public place like a pub or café. Then, prepare for things to get awkward. Meeting a new person is difficult enough when you share a common language. If you're stuttering your way through the first twenty minutes in German, just think ahead: soon, the tables will turn, and your partner will be stumbling through your native language. Tandem partners may not be for everybody, but they're a great way to learn German while gaining access to actual German people your age. Soon, you'll look forward to your tandem meet-ups, especially as communication gets easier. You may even get excited about learning a new grammar rule, as it will also promise a jump forward in your ability to understand your new friend.

Private tutors in Berlin can be surprisingly pricy, but are invaluable if you do not operate well in a group setting, or feel that your class is moving too quickly or too slowly for you. Private lessons may have their own set of intimidations (How to fill the entire lesson when you're the only one there?), but every student with the means would do well to try them. A private tutor will have the time to get to know you better than any of your previous teachers, and will not be as constrained by a lesson plan. A private tutor, for example, may immediately surmise that your vocabulary and grammar are already superior, but you lack the courage to use them. The answer will be several days of nothing but conversing, which will no doubt leave you with a splitting headache, but will also take you over that crucial hurdle between translating every sentence in your head and speaking without thinking. Most language schools also offer private tutoring, but if you want to find your own tutor in Berlin, websites like Erste Nachhilfe can help. A quick search of the English-language portal **Toytown Germany** may also yield tutor contacts directly from people who have used them.

Making German friends is still the best way to learn the language. >

WHAT'S NEXT?

If you've had about as much as you can take of German classes but you're still having trouble holding a conversation, don't despair. As with any professional instruction, these classes can only give you the tools you need to begin your mastery of the language; the rest lies with you. So be proactive in seeking out situations where you might be able to practice your language skills. If you have a job here, start by asking your colleagues to speak German around you more often, even if you have to respond in English. Spoken German can actually be fairly simple to understand, especially for a native English speaker. Its cadences can mimic English closely, and the two languages share many smaller, everyday words that tend to pop up a lot. Once you've begun to feel comfortable with this, ask a colleague or friend to act as the German half of the tandem partnership for you, sitting with you at lunch and letting you practice your German. Then, start asking some questions in the office or merely telling a lighthearted anecdote in the German you already know. Think of it as a fun game, rather than a strenuous test: how far into the story can you go, how many details can you add, when you're only telling it in German?

Consume as much embarrassingly lowbrow media as possible. Learning German gives you an excuse to read supermarket romance novels or kids' action comic books, or watch reality TV shows to your heart's content. Once you've grown weary of the easy stuff, move on to real news programs, newspapers, and websites like *Spiegel Online*. Even turning the radio on as you make breakfast in the morning can have a bigger impact than you might think: tune to Deutschlandfunk or RBB (Rundfunk Berlin Brandenburg) for news paired with culture and music. *Deutsch Perfekt* is an unintimidating magazine in German for those learning German. It gathers articles from real German newspapers and magazines of varying language levels and republishes them alongside small glossaries to help readers. Games and quizzes, although a bit juvenile at first, are also intended to get you reading in German as quickly as possible. An annual subscription also comes with free access to an online portal with many more games and interactive programs.

Strangely enough, one of your go-to writers for learning German may end up being **Shakespeare**. Find yourself a few worn copies of Shakespeare's most popular works in translation and you'll find, to your delight, that reading them in German is not at all difficult. You already know *Romeo and Juliet* or *Hamlet*, and this will free you to concentrate on vocabulary and sentence structure instead of trying to decipher the plot. Reading Shakespeare also promises an added bit of merriment: discovering how Germany has decided to translate some of the greatest lines in English literature. "Sein oder Nichtsein, das hier ist die Frage!"

Regardless of how you choose to begin your German language education, it is important to remember that learning any language is an ongoing process—one that can take a lifetime instead of a finite number of years. There is really no end to becoming fluent, as languages can change too. As long as you approach learning German with realistic expectations, and try not to compare yourself to those around you (there will always be someone better than you are, and many who are worse), you'll be able to enjoy an educational journey you are, in fact, very lucky to be on.

GETTING AROUND IN THE CITY

Depending on whom you ask, Berlin is either comfortably small or frighteningly large. You can traverse its center on a bicycle in less than an hour. S-Bahn and U-Bahn lines crisscross the city every few minutes in daytime. The more you get used to navigating the city, the smaller it will seem. The city's wide-open green spaces and vast empty lots (still visible, though dwindling) can make it seem far more spread out than any other capital, even though its population, as of the 2012 census, was around 3.3 million. Although you may become intimately familiar with the neighborhoods in which you live and work, the city is large enough, and still psychologically if not physically disjointed enough, to feel like a series of interconnected villages. You may never get to some of them simply because you have no business there, even after years of living in Berlin.

All wheels in Berlin are pretty reliable and quite useful if you know how to use them. What follows is an overview of Berlin's transportation options, so you can stop getting lost in your new city and start living in it.

The first time you use Berlin's **public transportation**, you may walk up or down a flight of stairs, look around for some kind of pay barrier before the platform, and then realize with glee that there is none. "Time to rejoice!" You'll think. "I heard Berlin would be awesome, but I didn't know it would also be free!" Relax: it's not free. It's merely somewhat backward in its payment methods, employing the honor system instead of making every rider pay up front. It is not alone: cities like Vienna, Budapest, or Prague still operate this way as well. The advantages for riders are manifold, the advantages for the system less so.

Most Berliners seem to like paying on the honor system as it saves time and allows them to be the master of their own fates. Recently, however, the BVG (Berliner Verkehrsbetriebe) has realized that it doesn't employ enough people to check the trains at random (in a so-called *Fahrscheinkontrolle*). Several annual price hikes in a row have only served to aggravate the local populace and underscore the feeling that the system is out of order. It may be a long time yet until Berlin decides to go the way of the western world and install pay barriers at every station. Until then, whether you buy a ticket or not, it pays to know your way around Berlin's public transportation system.

Your best resource for doing that is the **BVG's website**, one of the few websites from an official entity in Berlin that is also available in English. It gives you an overview of fares, downloadable transportation maps, and, in a stroke of genius, the so-called "journey planner." Here, you can enter your place of origin and destination, choose your modes of transport, and a page will pop up telling you the best routes and exactly how long they take. On weeknights, U- and S-Bahn lines stop running from around 1 am to 4:30 am, so if you're out at midnight on a weekday and want to know whether to rush, a quick check of the journey planner will tell you.

Berlin's public transport system consists of nine **U-Bahn** lines numbered 1 to 9 (if you don't count the U55, which

^ *The S-Bahn is a mixture of public and private city living.*

is actually just a separate branch of the U5 currently under construction) and 15 **S-Bahn** lines with slightly more confusing but ultimately arbitrary numbering. Some of these S-Bahn lines cross the city and meet at Friedrichstraße, while others circle the city in both directions as the Ringbahn. There are twenty-two tramlines, with those designated as **Metrotrams** running around the clock and more frequently. There are myriad bus lines in all parts of the city, and they can be intimidating at first, but take the time to get to know them: most have long routes that cover huge distances, making them a sometimes better (although slower) option than trains.

You'll see ticket machines at either end of every station platform and inside trams (tickets for buses can be bought from the driver). Next to these (or inside both trams and buses) are boxes with small slits, usually either red or yellow. They are your **ticket validating machines,** which stamp your ticket with the station, date, and time. If you buy a single ticket called an *Einzelfahrschein*, for example, it allows you to ride for 120 minutes, but only if you stamp it. There are, as you might imagine, many ways to get around all this, making sure you never get caught by a ticket controller (though it's getting harder). Some try stamping the back of the ticket instead of the front, thereby making it possible to use the ticket twice, and feigning ignorance if they get caught. Others pretend to speak only English when caught, although more bilingual ticket controllers are being hired, making this one hard to pull off. Ticket controllers appear to come from all walks of life—men and women, old and young—and from seemingly any ethnic background. They usually dress in plain clothes and have no identifiable markings aside from their ID, which they keep well hidden until they are doing a check. The only way to spot them is to look for odd couples: ticket controllers always work in pairs so they can cover both ends of a train car, keeping any ticketless miscreants from running out on them. So if you see two people chatting to each other on the platform with small shoulder bags (where they keep the machines they use to print fines) and immediately splitting up when the train arrives to enter by different doors, you'll know you've spotted a pair of ticket controllers. Of course, if you're already on the train without a ticket you probably won't see this in time.

Since they wait for the doors to close to announce their presence, sometimes approaching each person quietly so the rest of the train suspects nothing, you'll have very little chance of escaping. Don't worry, though: if you do get caught, the fine is only 40 Euros. You will probably get hauled off the train as they write you out a fine, and miss a few more trains to boot. Although the entire thing can be pretty embarrassing, keep in mind that if you do this, you'll be causing damage to more than just your pride: The BVG loses millions every year due to riders not paying to use the system, resulting in price hikes for everyone, including you.

Aside from **single ride** tickets, there are also **day passes** (only worth it if you'll be riding three times or more in a day), weekly passes (good for tourists, but not worth the price if you live here) and monthly passes or **_Monatskarten_**, by far the most reasonable option if you take public transport every day, or even just every weekday. If you buy what's called a **_Jahreskarte_** or year card, which is in fact twelve _Monatskarten_ paid in advance, you get a significant discount. A little-known secret is the **_Kurzstrecke_** ticket, which allows you to ride either three S- or U-Bahn stations, or six bus or tram stations at a reduced price. Children ride free until the age of six, and then can buy discounted **_Schüler_ tickets** while of school age. **Seniors** (65+) also receive discounts on year cards. These cards are valid on all forms of transportation mentioned above, and never need to be shown to board trams and trains. Buses, however, have a fairly loose policy with tickets: you are meant to show the driver your ticket, but he will barely even glance at it, making the check seem a bit superfluous. Ticket controllers can appear at any time, on any form of transportation of course, but they tend to stick with the options more people and especially more tourists use, and are rarely seen on buses and trams. Riders have reported an upswing in ticket checks on the first of the month, when controllers hope to catch those who forgot to buy a new _Monatskarte_. All the same, proceed with caution. Or better yet, with honesty.

One piece of advice: **get a bicycle**. If you're only traveling by U-Bahn, zipping around underground to emerge at different stations, you'll only have a mole's eye view of the city. A bike forces you to figure out a route from point A to point B, including all the unknown streets, confusing intersections, and perplexing parks in between. In contrast to many other cities where bikes and cars only attempt a symbiosis in daily life, in Berlin they have pretty much achieved it. That makes for an exhilarating experience: a form of open-air transportation fast enough to get you where you need to go if you're in a hurry, but slow enough that you'll also be able to coast along, enjoying the scenery.

But keep in mind that the reason the city is so bike-friendly, indeed the reason bikes manage to share the road with cars at all, is that there are so many rules and regulations governing their use. Claiming ignorance of the rules won't help if you break them, so keep a few things in mind when on two wheels. First and foremost, cyclists are required to obey all rules of the road, stopping at red lights and paying attention to signs just as a car driver would. Drivers in Berlin are generally pretty understanding towards cyclists as long as they don't do anything stupid, and that has something to do with the sheer prevalence of bicycles: even if you own a car, you probably own a bike as well. Bike paths are ubiquitous in Berlin and designated in a number of ways, so it will take seeing them several times before you recognize them automatically: they can be either a strip on the sidewalk in a different material (brick

against stone or concrete, for example) or separated from it with a stripe of paint in a different color (prevalent around building sites, where temporary bike paths may have been hastily drawn). They can also be on the street, painted on like car lanes and marked with the image of a bicycle. Bike paths are there for your safety, but don't make the mistake of feeling so safe as to become complacent. The biggest threats to cyclists on a bike path, besides another bicycle going the wrong way (also a big no-no) are pedestrians; mostly tourists who don't recognize what they're standing on. Cyclists, of course, can also do a lot of harm to pedestrians as well.

Bikes need to be decked out and geared up, especially in springtime and early summer when the police are out in force trying to catch anyone who didn't bring his two-wheeler in for a **post-winter tune-up**. Make sure you have reflectors at front and back and on both wheels, and at least one hand break that works, along with a working bell. Make sure you have back (red) and front (white) lights on your bike. Frowned upon is talking on your mobile phone or riding while listening to music via headphones or earbuds (they are not forbidden, however, but you have to be able to listen for traffic). Riding drunk, while obviously dangerous, will not get you into nearly as much trouble as driving drunk (especially since most drunks on bikes are probably on their way home at 3 in the morning, with very few people around to witness their swerving). Still, police sometimes stake out a street corner late at night for exactly this purpose, so monitor your drinks if you're biking home; you'll have to be your own designated driver.

Helmets are not required but are, as ever, an extremely good idea. The increasing number of construction sites in town means that whole street sections are being closed off, with bicycles and cars rerouted into a single lane too small for both. It takes only a quick misjudgment to get side-swiped by a passing bus, for example, and car drivers tend to be more frazzled and less self-aware when navigating makeshift lanes through construction sites. A lot of Berliners have noticed this lately and taken proper precaution, leading to an upswing in the number of bikers wearing helmets.

Bikes can be taken on most forms of public transportation. Nearly every car of the S-Bahn has designated bike com-

< Cycling over the famous Oberbaumbrücke

partments, with rows of seats that fold up to make space for multiple bikes. You can also take your bike on the U-Bahn as long you're not taking the first car or riding during rush hour. Make sure you buy a special bike ticket (*Fahrradausweis*) and validate it. If you're found without one, it will result in the same 40-Euro fine you'd get if you were caught without a normal ticket.

The **ADFC** or Allgemeiner Deutscher Fahrrad Club is a German biking club that offers a range of services, including bi-annual free check-up stations throughout the city, classes, area maps, and books. A membership offers all kinds of discounts and freebies for avid bikers, as well as automatic liability, legal, and theft insurance. It costs 46 Euros per year for an adult of 27 or older, or 56 Euros per year for the entire family.

Although Craigslist is a terrible place to find apartments, it is actually quite a good place to troll for cheap **second-hand bicycles**, as many temporary Berliners use the site to get rid of theirs before leaving town. If you plan on scouring the flea markets but want assurance that you aren't buying stolen goods, you certainly won't get it at Mauerpark or Treptower Park. In fact, some of these flea markets have become so notorious as stolen bike markets, there's a well-known saying: if your bike gets stolen on Saturday night from Kottbusser Tor, you can probably buy it back again on Sunday morning at Treptower Park. Still, there are deals to be had from among the wrecks and rust-buckets, as long as you can speak a bit of German, know a bit about bikes, and like to bargain. For everyone else, there are straightforward, goodie-two-shoes bike shops, where you'll find every kind of bike at every price. But try to resist the urge to plunk down several hundred Euros for a painted Dutch bike with a leather saddle, wicker basket, and, expensive lights. Everyone in Berlin has an equal chance of getting a bike stolen at some point, but you greatly up your chances and your grief by buying the nicest one around. Even your dream bike will get scuffed quickly if you use it often; better to have something ugly and reliable than beautiful and gone.

Although Berlin is a bike-friendly city, it's also full of cars, and sooner or later, you may want to get one too. The advantages of **owning a car** in Berlin are manifold, but so are the disadvantages. The greatest limitation you'll face is that of space: zipping around the city in an *Auto* can be fun, but you may end up wasting as much time as you save in the endless search for parking. Residency permits allowing you to park in your *Kiez* are available at the same place you register your address, the *Einwohnermeldeamt*, but they're no guarantee against all available parking spaces being taken by your neighbors. Metered parking is ubiquitous, but can really add up if you use it all the time. Garages are pricy and not all that prevalent. If you own a car in Berlin, the best thing to do is find a place where it can stay long-term, only breaking it out for special occasions like *Tagesausflüge* (day trips) or if your best friends need help moving (trust me, they'll ask). Of course, the parking situation doesn't stop Berliners from driving, nor should it. Berliners can be aggressive drivers, but the roads are regulated enough that the situation never really gets out of hand. Traffic accidents, especially ones that lead to injury, are relatively low for the population, and cars obey speed limits within the city, choosing instead to let loose on the *Autobahn* where speed limits are usually mere suggestions.

All driver's licenses are valid in Germany for up to six months from date of entry. If you want to stay for longer than six months but less than a year, you can have your permission extended by your local registration office. If you have moved here for good, however, you'll need to exchange your old license for a German license, or **Führerschein**. (The name can be confusing and a little unfortunate, with "*Führer*" in this case meaning the operator of a vehicle and not a certain German dictator.) Whether you can do this easily, however, depends on which country, and even which US state, you come from. If you are an EU citizen, you can simply continue driving with a valid license from your home country. If you are not, you must find out whether your home country has a reciprocity agreement with Germany. Germany has such agreements with Japan, Korea, Israel, South Africa, New Zealand, and Australia, as well as most Canadian provinces.

Germany only has reciprocity agreements with some US states, so depending on which state issued your driver's license, you're in for either a quick trip to the registration office, or several weeks and several hundred Euros in costs—first to take the required driving classes (even if you know how to drive) and then to pass the written and practical examinations. Even if you come from a country that has a reciprocity agreement, give yourself some time to gather the required documents (an application must include your valid home license translated into German, a service best done by **ADAC**, the Allgemeiner Deutscher Automobil-Club). In some cases you will also need an eye exam and a certificate from a first aid course, although, as with applying for a visa, these requirements seem to vary depending on whom you ask. Give your local registration office ample time as well, since all too often, the people at these offices simply don't know which countries have valid reciprocity agreements with Germany, or what to do to switch a foreign license into a local one. As with the *Ausländerbehörde*, to avoid being given the runaround, show up with more paperwork than you think you'll need.

Once you have your driver's license, you may wish you'd taken a special class in **German driving**. While the thought of driving at near racecar speeds on the *Autobahn* can strike fear into the hearts of even the most seasoned motorists, the rest of Germany's roads are pretty civil in comparison, governed by a complicated set of rules that, much like the German language, seem to have endless exceptions. The most important and easy-to-remember one is the so-called ***Rechts vor Links*** or "right before left" rule. This states that, on any street not designated as having right of way (*Vorfahrtstraßen*, marked by a yellow diamond within a white one), you must always yield to traffic from your right. Speed limits within urban areas are almost always 50 km per hour, unless posted otherwise (certain residential streets, for example, are marked as *Verkehrsberuhigte Zone* or calm traffic zones). Cameras, radar, and policemen seem to be everywhere, however, even hiding in the bushes waiting to collect fines, so try to obey the rules to the best of your ability. Most policemen, like most motorists, won't be so understanding if you try to explain that you simply didn't know.

If you are caught speeding, often by radar-controlled cameras planted at specific points, a ticket and money transfer slip will be sent to your home. In case of an accident, you are of course required to stay at the scene, exchange insurance details with the other motorist, and call the police to file an official report. In addition, German motorists are required to drive with both a first aid kit and warning triangle to set up on the road if their car should break down. All drivers are also required to carry not only their license and registration but also documentation of car insurance (*Kraftfahrzeugversicherung*).

If you've ever gotten into a conversation with a German about driving, you'll probably hear some mumbling about **Punkte (points) in Flensburg**. Flensburg is an actual city in northern Germany where the German department of motor vehicles (*Kraftfahrzeugamt*) is located, and where your driving record is kept. Crimes, misdemeanors, and even minor mistakes on the road are categorized by severity, with most resulting in a fine and some in points added to your license in Flensburg. The more points you have, the worse it is, and 18 points can get your driver's license revoked indefinitely. Points under the dreaded 18, however, can be reduced by taking a driving improvement course that is either voluntary or mandatory, depending on your tally. Also, Flensburg may be the only point system where biking rules apply as well. Although unlikely, it is technically possible to earn points in Flensburg from biking while talking on your mobile phone or biking drunk.

The first thing you should know when **buying a car** in Berlin is that the city has had an environmental protection fine in place since January of 2008. This means that any car driving within the Ringbahn must be environmentally friendly, and must display a green sticker declaring it so. Also in keeping with Berlin's pollution law is the German propensity for buying small cars. It isn't just the lack of parking in the city, but a high level of environmental awareness that keeps car sizes convenient. The gas-guzzlers Americans increasingly favor are still looked down upon here, and sputtering, polluting old engines are entirely outlawed. Here, the size of your car is not quite as important as things like safety and drivability, and smaller options like Minis and Smarts join classic German brands like Volkswagen and BMW on the road, along with a smaller percentage of foreign brands. The idea of the "family van" is virtually nonexistent here, as parents are much more likely to transport their tots to Kindergarten in what's called a

Kinderanhänger, a tent-like contraption that attaches to a bike. Gas is also quite expensive, making it difficult for couples or families to afford anything more than a modest vehicle.

Buying a car in Germany is one of the easiest things to do as a foreigner. There are numerous car dealerships to be found in the industrial areas lining the Ringbahn, and a good many in the eastern part of Moabit bordering Charlottenburg. If you want a unique experience, order a Volkswagen and pick it up at the Autostadt in Wolfsburg—basically a car-lover's version of Disneyland, complete with interactive exhibits, a hotel, restaurants, a performing arts program, and a museum of cars through the ages—built by Volkswagen of course, as a monument to itself. As with apartments, cars also have their own websites. Check **mobil.de** for cars sorted by make, mileage, and dealership location, or **autoscout24.de** (the automobile version of immobilienscout) to buy second-hand cars directly from current owners.

Car sharing options are becoming increasingly prevalent in Berlin, and are a great, low-cost option for those who do not wish to commit to a vehicle. Far from posing a threat to big car companies, these programs are mostly sponsored by them, as they've come to realize the appeal of more flexible options to young city-dwellers.

DriveNow, a cooperation between BMW and the rental company Sixt, and Car2Go from Daimler both offer mobile phone accessibility for booking on the go as well as user-friendly websites.

Citroën Multicity is the first car sharing option in Germany with exclusively electric cars. It is a partnership with Flinkster, the station-based car sharing company run by Deutsche Bahn.

BERLIN WITH KIDS

Moving to Berlin with kids. It may not be the easiest thing you'll ever do, but once you're on the ground, the advantages will quickly outnumber the obstacles. If you're a parent already, this is probably old news to you, but kids have a way of breaking down barriers and allowing us to overcome fears—even those we may carry as adults. If you've just moved here and feel lost in a foreign country, watch your kids make friends for you as they approach shopkeepers on the street, dog owners in parks, or other kids on playgrounds, even those with whom they share no common language. Follow your kids' example, and you may find yourself melting easily into their social networks, allowing their favorite haunts to become yours. Your kids will probably be acting like locals long before you do, so you could do worse than let them show you the way.

Of course, moving to a foreign country is not for the faint of heart. And moving with children should earn you some kind of medal. If you're a parent, you shouldn't kid yourself (no pun intended) about the added complexities of life with kids in Berlin. On the other hand, relax: There's a reason *Kinder*, the German word for children, seems to show up all over town: Berlin is as child-friendly as cities can be. If you've got a problem or question about your child, there's probably an entire *Amt* dedicated to helping you. In a country known for its bureaucracy, being a parent can help you see the good side of all the paperwork: a great support network and a little peace of mind.

A WORD ABOUT GERMANY'S *KINDER* SITUATION

Like most post-industrial, developed nations, Germany has a bit of a **birth rate problem** (though you wouldn't know it from traipsing around Prenzlauer Berg). According to an article in the *Guardian* in 2012, Germany's birthrate is actually the lowest in Europe, and one of the lowest in the world. A combination of longer study periods, more women seeking careers, and the general, 21st century trend towards starting families later and keeping them smaller has resulted in Germany's mere 663,000 births in 2012. It isn't difficult to see the problem: a declining workforce and an aging population will lead to an economic conundrum for a country that has long prided itself on its social services. With more people dying than being born, it is conceivable—and actually quite likely—that in a few generations, government-sponsored social funds like health insurance and retirement will reach the point of no return. In fact, that's why a neighborhood like Prenzlauer Berg, often chided for its clichéd version of German upper-middle class privilege, should actually be lauded as the birthplace of Germany's future saviors.

Of course, this *Kinder* shortage spells good news for Berlin parents: a wealth of services here are designed to make the idea of having children more attractive to those who may think twice about its financial toll. First and foremost among these is **Kindergeld**. If you know even a bit of German, you'll probably recognize the word tacked onto the back of that compound: *Geld* or money. *Kindergeld* is officially known as a "child benefit," but it's actually a parent benefit—not a lot, but at least a bit of financial support, making it easier to budget for child essentials like diapers, food, and clothing. In order to receive Kindergeld, parents and their children must merely provide proof of German residency—they must not necessarily be German citizens. A **Kinderzuschlag** or additional children's allowance is also applicable to low-income parents who can prove that their monthly income falls within a certain bracket. Parents who take advantage of this extra children's allowance can also receive additional support for things like school supplies, after-school activities, and transfers to and from school.

An equally generous companion to *Kindergeld*, the *Eltern-geld* scheme is nothing to scoff at, allowing parents to take time off from work or **Elternzeit** at a substantial percentage of their normal income: 67% of after-tax earnings calculated in the 12 months before the birth of the child, capped at 1,800 Euros per month. In other cities that may seem like a pittance, but in Berlin it is enough to live on. It is also is quite a nice supplement to a dual-income household, enabling a parent to spend time with a new baby without putting the family in dire straits. This system may not have reached the gender equality of the Netherlands or Scandinavia, where new fathers and mothers take nearly equal time off, but it still allows for splitting time between two partners: single parents receive 14 months of payment, whereas couples receive 12 months for the initial caregiver and an additional 2 months for the spouse or partner. When receiving *Elterngeld*, you are even permitted to continue working fewer than 30 hours a week. Just be aware that the money you make may be deducted from your *Elterngeld* and is also taxable. Although this system is centered on those who have full-time jobs (presumably paying into the social system for years already) you can still receive *Elterngeld* even if you're never worked in Germany; it is simply calculated based on your former wages in your home country. Even if you're a freelancer, you can calculate it based on your income in the year prior to your child's birth, and prove it when applying with your *Steuererklärung* or tax return.

In Berlin, Prenzlauer Berg still remains the most famous of the "**baby boom**" neighborhoods, with Kreuzberg, Friedrichshain, and even Neukölln following close behind. Here you will find the highest number of like-minded parents, playgrounds, cafes and shops dedicated to children, and of course, daycare spots. Keep in mind, though, that the relative baby-friendliness of these areas means that most other Berlin parents probably had the same idea you did, resulting in a lot of competition over resources. Just because Prenzlauer Berg has some kind of daycare option on every block doesn't mean you won't have trouble finding space for your child there. You'll just have a lot of other parents to commiserate with.

Next page: It feels like a baby boom every summer: swimming at Groß Glienecker See, a big lake at the city limits.

VARIOUS TYPES OF *KITAS* AND SCHOOLS

If you come from an English-speaking country, you probably remember going to something called "kindergarten." By now perhaps you've realized that word is German. In Germany, Kindergarten can be quite different from the regimented entry year into the school system you experienced. In fact, there is no version of German Kindergarten. Affectionately referred to as *Kita* (for **Kindertagestätte** or child daycare), these first few years of education and development are seen as absolutely crucial. What kind of *Kita* you choose for your kids can say a lot about your parenting style. Strangely enough, however, though school attendance in Germany is compulsory, *Kitas* are not part of the school system and are therefore less uniform. While this means you'll have more options when it comes to daycare, it has also led to a severe shortage of *Kita* places. This in turn has fueled a government crusade to ensure each child over the age of one a place at some kind of daycare center. This may work in theory, but in practice it still means competition: just because a place somewhere in the city has been ensured for your child doesn't mean it will be the place you want. In all cases, it helps to make friends with your local *Jugendamt* (children's board), which will give you what's called a *Kitagutschein* (a voucher for attending Kindergarten) as well as access to private services (if you want to go this route) and general advice about getting on waitlists for them.

The earliest options for your child will be either a *Kinderkrippe* (literally "children's crib") or a *Tagesmutter* ("day mother"). You can start your children with these in infancy, going up to the age of about three, when your child has the option to enter the public *Kita* system (the word "public" in this case does not mean that the *Kitas* are government-run, but rather that they are funded according to income and overseen by the *Jugendamt.*). **Kinderkrippe** are simply a version of *Kita*, geared towards the youngest children. A **Tagesmutter** can be public (government-regulated and assigned by the *Jugendamt*) or private (chosen by you, with price and times negotiated according to your needs and her availability). Much like babysitters or au pairs, *Tagesmutter* care can vary widely according to the personality of the caregiver and what she believes to be best for children. Exercise due diligence here: you probably won't want a *Tagesmutter* with a parenting style markedly different from yours. You may also have heard of **Kinderläden**. These are exactly what they sound like: neighborhood storefronts or *Läden* made up to be mini kindergartens. These are alternatives to state-regulated *Kitas* and not free, but they represent yet another option in the ongoing search for the right place and care.

Once your child has turned three, you will most likely want to have him or her attend *Kita*, ideally within a short walk from where you live. Due to the scarcity of *Kita* spots, some say it is advisable to start looking for adequate facilities and putting your child on waiting lists while you are still pregnant. This may seem perverse to some parents, but the competition is fierce. Not all *Kitas* will accept applications before the child is born, but some will, so it is best to make up a list of those that interest you most and simply call. A good resource for finding *Kitas* categorized by Berlin districts is Kita.de.

As early as nine months before you plan to start your child in *Kita*, apply for your **Kitagutschein** at the *Jugendamt*. In order to do this, you will need to fill out a great number of confusing forms. Again, it is best to bring a bilingual friend or partner along to help (the *Jugendamt*, like most official Berlin bureaus, will be unlikely to have an English speaker on staff). The *Jugendamt* will determine how many hours of childcare you have a legal right to based on your working hours and your commute. It will also determine how much money you owe for childcare—something that is based on income rather than the attractiveness of the *Kita* or the relative expense of a certain neighborhood. If you enter your child into the public system, you'll be paying the *Jugendamt* directly, not the *Kita*. Once your child reaches the age of three, he or she is entitled to seven hours of *Kita* daily, regardless of your work circumstances. In addition, a new law passed in 2009 makes the three years of public *Kita* leading up to school free in Berlin (not counting fees for meals, or extra care outside of normal *Kita* hours).

You'll find that a good *Kita* will be like an extended family: *Kitas* routinely host parties, fairs, and family events, ask for parental input and take it seriously, and even organize day and overnight trips for the kids. But don't forget that *Kita* is still more or less a business, and as such needs to make sure it allots resources adequately: don't be surprised if your *Kita* closely monitors when you drop off and pick up your child, and admonishes you if you go over your time allotment. The last thing they (and you) want is a lot of overworked and dissatisfied people taking care of your children, so *Kitas* have to make sure there are enough caregivers (almost always women called *Erzieherinnen*) for the number of children there at any time.

Once you have your *Kita* voucher, you are eligible for a *Kita* spot, and can legally sign a contract with one when the time comes. If you do not plan on entering your child into the public system, but rather want to look for a more specialized, private *Kita*, you can expect a wide range of options but higher fees. There are a great number of **bilingual *Kitas*** in Berlin, for example, but they fill up quickly, as international parents who want their kids speaking both languages also have to compete with ambitious German families. For a more alternative approach to early education, there are several Waldorf kindergartens sprinkled all over Berlin, and a bilingual Montessori preschool in the vicinity of Dahlem. The Montessori *Kinderhäuser* (children's houses) are a number of Montessori *Kitas* scattered across West Berlin that feed directly into the IMS Internationale Montessorischule, an all-day elementary school or *Grundschule* in Wannsee. The so-called *Waldkita* is a Scandinavian concept that allows children to learn while traipsing around the forest or outdoors. The website for Germany's Association of Nature and Forest Kindergartens (bvnw.de) provides a list of them. There are also a good number of Catholic and Protestant *Kitas* in Berlin, but these are considered part of the public school system (Catholic and Protestant churches being publicly funded), teach in much the same manner as a normal *Kita*, and do not have any religious requirements for acceptance.

Once your child has reached the age of six or so, he or she can begin attending **Grundschule** or elementary school. There is a bit of wiggle room, however, in that many schools institute a summer cut-off date. A child whose sixth birthday is before this date (in other words, already six or turning six over the summer) is called a *Muss-Kind* (literally a "must" child) and is obligated to start school. A child who turns six after this date is called a *Kann-Kind* (a "can" child), and parents may decide whether to send him or her to school or back to *Kita* for one last year. This decision is not one made lightly, as it often involves a good grasp of the child's social development much more than any assumption about intelligence: a conscientious, outgoing child might appear to be ready for school, but might benefit even more from that last year in kindergarten. In any case, *Grundschule* lasts four years in most of Germany, six years in Berlin and Brandenburg, and consists of a classic western education (reading, writing, 'rithmetic in addition to science, history and optional religion). It goes from about 8 in the morning until 1 or 2 in the afternoon, although some schools are instituting full-day classes in response to a greater number of parents wishing to rejoin the workforce.

The most important thing you'll need to know about your child's first year of *Grundschule*, however, has absolutely nothing to do with school itself. Rather, it is the **Einschulung** or "first day of school" party, a rather charming German tradition in which parents throw a party for the pupil-to-be, showering him or her with gifts that include school supplies, toys, and a whole lot of candy, all packed into a *Schultüte* or "school cone," a colorful paper and cardboard cone. Don't even think about skipping this, even if your child is not German: a six year old will be perceptive enough to know when he isn't getting something all the other kids are, and conveniently "forgetting" the *Einschulung* party would be the equivalent of forgetting a birthday. If you live in a child-rich neighborhood, plan early. Around the beginning of August, when the school year starts after *Sommerferien* (summer holidays), every café, restaurant, and outdoor space will be booked out for an *Einschulung*. This does not have to be an elaborate affair, but rather can be a simple coffee-and-cake date with family or some of the child's closest friends.

After *Grundschule*, children have traditionally been split up according to a **three-tiered system** that is regarded by some as controversial, by others as the veritable backbone of German society. According to how well a child has done in school, a parent will decide to enroll him or her in **Gymnasium**,

Realschule, or *Hauptschule*. The first is considered the most prestigious, putting students on track to take what's called an Abitur exam, thereby gaining a diploma that will allow them entry to German universities. With this type of schooling, students choose a specific focus (math and science, for example, or literature and humanities) quite early on, and graduate at around 18 or 19. *Realschule*, the second option, is still quite respected and popular in Germany, offering students a rigorous academic education in conjunction with more specific training in preparation for a trade, including high level business work. Students take the *Realabschluss* to graduate at the end of the tenth year, at which point they may go on to a *Berufsschule* or technical school combining further study with vocational training and an apprenticeship. *Hauptschule* is considered the lowest tier, preparing students for work in specific trades with a program that combines schooling with a part-time apprenticeship. Upon completion, students can take the *Hauptschulabschluss* exam or go on to the *Realschulabschluss* depending on grades and accomplishments.

Now, if it seems unfair to determine a child's entire life based on his academic accomplishments before the age of twelve, that's because it is. Many feel that the three-tiered system produces results that conflict dramatically with what was intended; namely, a highly-democratic, classless system that evaluates each student according to academic performance instead of a host of other factors like connections and family income. Ideally, a high-performing student from a wealthy family attending an excellent *Grundschule* in Zehlendorf, for instance, should have the same chance of getting into a good Gymnasium as a high-performing student from a working class, immigrant family attending an underprivileged *Grundschule* in Neukölln. Of course, this ends up ignoring the many other factors that can affect a student's overall performance, such as a family's financial situation, whether a student faces peer pressure or even violence in schools, and whether the student himself possesses the will to study.

In practice, however, the system is not quite as strict and thankless as it might seem. Students receive their grades, backed up by unofficial teacher recommendations. Besides the official grade slip, there will be no written statement about the future prospects of the student, from the school or its teachers. This means that, while parents are free to discuss their child's future with teachers, those teachers have no power other than to state an opinion. If parents feel strongly that their child, a decent but not outstanding student, should try for *Gymnasium* instead of enrolling in *Hauptschule* or *Realschule*, they are free to seek out a *Gymnasium* that will accept their child. Moreover, once *Hauptschule* or *Realschule* students have finished their schooling, and later on decide they are still interested in a university degree, they are entitled to two years of evening training to help them obtain their *Abitur* so that they may enroll in university after all.

On top of all this, in recent years the inherent unfairness many see in this three-tiered system has perhaps been met with an adequate answer: the so-called **Gesamtschule**, which incorporates elements of all three tracks into a teaching method that acknowledges and attempts to build on differences among students. The idea, at least according to the official Berlin website Berlin.de, is to develop "eine Schule für Alle" or "a school for everybody". Only time will tell whether this catchphrase comes to represent an entirely new and democratic educational method for Germany or remains a mere slogan used to quell parental fears.

There are several respected **international schools** in Berlin:
*   The **John F. Kennedy School** is a public school mostly for students of bilingual German-English backgrounds, with children of US diplomats and other officials receiving top priority. Third-party nationals can apply as well, with the understanding that they'll probably be on a waitlist for quite a while. JFK preps students for either a typical liberal arts college education in America or a university education in Germany.
*   The **Nelson Mandela School** in Wilmersdorf offers a "Flex" concept in the early years adjusted to each child's development and language skills.
*   The **Quentin Blake Europe School** in Dahlem
*   The **Charles Dickens Primary School** in Grunewald
*   The **Berlin Brandenburg International School** in Zehlendorf

These schools all offer a bilingual education in varying forms, but only some of them give children the training they need to reenter the school system successfully somewhere along the line back home; something to consider for parents who are not planning on staying in Germany for the duration of their child's education.

BABYSITTERS AND AU PAIRS

Unsurprisingly in a city like Berlin, where plenty of young people are looking for part-time work, babysitters and au pairs are not that hard to come by. If you would like to hire a **babysitter**, it is best to start within your own trusted networks: ask parents at your *Kita* whether they know anyone who has used a good babysitter in the past, or if their babysitter might be interested in picking up extra work. You might also consider posting on expat websites such as Craigslist or ExBerliner if you are looking for a non-German babysitter, or on announcement boards of local high schools or universities if you are looking for a native German speaker.

An **au pair** is generally a young adult past schooling age who accepts a salary plus room and board in exchange for work as a live-in nanny. In Germany, the family hiring an au pair is generally expected to have at least one German parent, since part of the au pair experience (and one of the reasons Germany grants one-year visas solely for au pairs) is learning the language of his or her host country and family. According to a new law, however, exceptions can be made if a non-German family wishes to hire an au pair whose native language is anything other than the family's own.

Websites like **AuPairWorld** or **EasyAuPair** offer listings in English and take care of all details of the au pair transaction. Host families are encouraged, but not required, to shepherd their au pair through the visa process, providing a job description and official contract. Au pairs in Germany are expected to have some prior knowledge of the German language, but if they intend to work solely in English, they can also get away with taking a German class outside of working hours in order to cover this requirement.

The host family should also take into account a range of extras, such as paying for the au pair's health insurance and granting vacation days, but the consensus is that these are not as regulated as they should be. If you are a host family, try to foresee the needs and wishes of your potential au pair: the au pair-host relationship is not intended to be one-sided, but rather as a cultural exchange that is equally beneficial to both parties.

DOCTORS AND EMERGENCY SERVICES IN BERLIN

The last thing you want in a foreign country is to be stuck with a sick kid and not a trusted doctor in sight. The best advice is to go about finding a pediatrician you like at around the same time you're figuring out your family's German health insurance. That way you'll already have someone you know and trust—with any luck, just around the corner.

English-speaking pediatricians in Berlin are not that numerous, but neither are English-speaking doctors of any sort. You can get a head start by using the website Kinderärzte-im-Netz (www.kinderaerzteimnetz.de/berlin). The US Embassy also has a list of both hospitals and doctors offering adequate care in English, and includes a section on pediatricians. It can be found at the following link: germany.usembassy.gov/germany/img/assets/9057/berlin_medical.pdf

Germans these days, especially in Berlin, seem to come hard-wired with a suspicion of classical forms of medicine (the so-called Schulmedizin system). This means they are much more likely to demand natural, herbal, and homeopathic remedies than, say, Americans. This is good news if you are also of the opinion that western society is over-medicated, but it may mean doing due diligence if you automatically want the same kind of care you might find at home.

In general, pediatricians are a bit more amenable to helping out in an emergency than adult doctors, and offer friendlier service and quicker response times. If your child has a condition for which you cannot find an adequate doctor in time, Charité, the big university hospital in Berlin, has a number of clinics for children and adolescents spread out across its campuses in Mitte, Wedding, Buch and Steglitz. St. Joseph-

Krankenhaus in Tempelhof also offers extensive services for children through its *Kinderklinik*.

WHAT TO DO WITH KIDS IN BERLIN

You may blissfully remember a time before your life was filled with bureaucracy, unhelpful school officials, and trips to the *Jugendamt*. Now that you've settled in, found the proper school and the best doctor for your kids, and gotten comfortable with your routine, that dream may once again become reality. Sure, you now have some free time to spend with your kids again, but how do you keep them entertained in a city you—and they—might not be entirely familiar with? Never fear: Berlin's **Kindercafés** are here!

- **Milchbart** on Paul-Robeson-Straße is like a *Kita*-away-from-*Kita*, offering a brightly painted play space for kids and child-friendly activities like knitting classes or even a weekly English class.
- **Niesen** on Schwedter Straße is a largely unrenovated space that harks back to the early days of post-Wall Prenzlauer Berg, with enough space for kids to run around while parents sip coffee with other parents.
- **Kiezkind** and **Das Spielzimmer** anchor two ends of Helmholtzplatz in Prenzlauer Berg.
- **Paul und Paula** offers a haven for Friedrichshain's parents, with a café that doubles as an activity center while also serving up child-friendly treats.
- **Rudimarie** on Neukölln's Weichselplatz is not a *Kindercafé* per se, but has become one automatically due to its location around the corner from one playground and right across from another.

While most cities have a token children's museum, Berlin has several **Kindermuseen**; some with fairly conventional settings, others so wild and creative they could hardly be called "museums" at all:
- The **Labyrinth Kindermuseum** in Wedding is arguably the best, a 1000-square meter former factory turned into a

cross between an interactive museum, play space, learning center, and children's dream world.

- The **MachMit** (literally "make with" or "participate") *Kindermuseum* on Senefelderplatz has been providing an outlet for child creativity for more than twenty years now.
- The **Familienfarm Lübars** is an interactive farm for parents and their kids as well as school groups in the village of Lübars in northern Reinickendorf.
- **Museumsdorf Düppel** is an interactive "museum village" mimicking medieval times on the site of an actual 13th century settlement. Kids are guided by volunteers in costume, and can try out woodworking and pottery on antique machines and play medieval games among the "historical" houses.
- Museum **Domäne Dahlem** is an open-air museum of agrarian history on the site of the former Dahlem manor, complete with an organic farm and market. Here, children can interact with animals, pick fruit in season, and learn about how food travels from farm to table.
- **Naturschutzzentrum Ökowerk** in Grunewald is an interactive center on the grounds of a former water plant offering kids a close-up look at nature and conservation, complete with ponds, gardens, forest paths, and a pitch-black underground water collection chamber with amazing acoustics.
- The **Jugendfarm Moritzhof** offers children interactive playtime with gentle animals a bit closer to home: at the northern end of Mauerpark.
- The **Jugendmuseum** (Youth Museum) Schöneberg encourages hands-on experimentation from children of all ages through workshops, improvised theater sketches, and other creative projects.

Some museums in Berlin, although not technically children's museums, are still wonderful and fascinating places to spend an afternoon, and welcome both children and adults alike. The **Deutsches Technikmuseum** Berlin, located on the banks of the Landwehrkanal just south of Potsdamer Platz, is an airplane or train geek's dream: on the grounds of Anhalter Bahnhof's former train depot, it contains exhibitions of planes, boats, and trains throughout the ages. The museum even has

Next page: The biggest playground of them all is former Tempelhof airport, now a gigantic park.

grounds featuring two historic windmills, a smithy and a brewery in a four-story brick building with a thrilling view of the overground U-Bahn lines passing by. The **Berlin Zoo and Aquarium** are a delight at any age, in the center of town, and large enough to fill an entire day of exploring. On rainy days, the **Naturkundemuseum** (natural history museum) is full of children and parents gazing in wonder at dinosaur bones, fossils, gems and minerals, and weird specimens in jars.

Practically every park and square in Berlin will have at least one *Spielplatz* (playground) if not more, and there are also some great smaller playgrounds simply tucked in between buildings. To keep up with Berlin's exploding *Kinder* population, playgrounds are being renovated, created, and expanded constantly. If you come from a country where child safety is taken a bit too seriously, though, to the point that all the adventure of childhood is taken out of the equation, you'll be pleasantly surprised by Germany's playgrounds, some of which may leave parents horrified even as their kids feel they've gone to *Spielplatz* heaven.

- **Kolle 37** at Senefelderplatz is an interactive playground founded by Prenzlauer Berg parents soon after the Wall fell. There, children can build huts, cook food on fires they've started, mold and fire pottery in kilns, and learn blacksmithing. Squeamish parents are advised to look away rather than trying to prevent their kids from going to this neighborhood institution.
- The modern playground at the new **Park am Gleisdreieck** includes trampolines, rope bridges, slides, and swings in different shapes and sizes.
- Sprawling gardens like the **Botanical Gardens** in Dahlem or the **Britzer Garten** in south Neukölln are also great picnicking and play spots for families, and often have events geared toward kids and their parents.
- In winter when Charlottenburg's **Lietzensee** freezes solid, kids can join the fearless multitudes that use the slick surface for skating, sledding, and even ice hockey.

STUDENT LIFE IN BERLIN

Berlin is quite an exciting place to be a student, and Berlin's students make up a sizable minority (140,000 according to Berlin.de). Its quality infrastructure makes it easy to live anywhere in town and still get to class on time. Its low-cost housing options mean that students can work a bit while studying and still manage to pay their rent. Its wealth of culture and leisure activities provides a much-needed balance between work and play. Practically every business in town offers student discounts: film, theater, and museum tickets can be purchased at discounted prices. The BVG allows university students to ride for only a fraction of the normal price on what's called a *Semesterticket.*

As a foreigner, you may feel like you're at a disadvantage when applying to study, but most of Berlin's schools are happy to accept non-Germans, reserving a number of spots for them (15%, according to Berlin.de). Many offer dedicated offices with open hours where you can come for advice, even as a prospective student, and an assessment of your qualifications. Helpful webpages in English guide non-German students in understanding the requirements and the application process, and some even have programs entirely in English that will have a mixture of international students and Germans with a high level of English competence. Their online student hub www.studentenwerk-berlin.de has a section in English dedicated to international students. Uni-Assist, the official university application service for international students, is used by nearly every Berlin university. In addition to offering a list of all universities it works with in Germany and downloadable application forms, Uni-Assist also publishes introductory information about degrees, expected application fees, and the application process.

If you make the decision to study in Berlin, you'll likely encounter an academic system that is distinctly German in its order and complexity. Educate yourself about the options available in order to make the best decision. It is also worthwhile to assess your reasons for studying. If you feel that you need a German degree to be eligible in the German job market, you might want to talk to professionals in the field you hope to go into: while more and more companies expect Germans to apply with a combined Bachelor's/Master's degree (more on that later), many of them will understand that academic requirements can be completely different elsewhere. A Bachelor's degree from a respected non-German university may be enough to get you in the door of a company badly in need of employees with second language skills. Many new, international startups and agencies may not care what kind of degree you have, as long as you bring new and valuable ideas with you. That being said, Germans take studying and academic degrees extremely seriously. Those with a "Dr." or "Prof." added to their name (of which there can be more than one, leading to somewhat hilarious titles like Prof. Dr. Dr. Schneider) will find that it opens many doors.

BERLIN'S UNIVERSITIES AND WHAT THEY OFFER

In addition to four universities and a university hospital, Berlin also boasts an impressive number of technical schools (so-called Hochschulen, not to be confused with the English word "high school," though this is its literal translation), art schools (Kunsthochschulen), and schools for applied science (Fachhochschulen). Neighboring Potsdam also has its own university, the largest in Brandenburg. Knowing where they are, their history, and what makes each of them special is crucial to understanding Berlin's academic landscape.

Humboldt-Universität (HU) is one of the oldest and most prestigious universities in Germany. Although its schools are scattered across the city, most people picture the stately Prussian halls lining either side of Unter den Linden just before

Museum Island. The first building to house the university was a palace built by Friedrich the Great as a location for parties and events, then donated by Friedrich Wilhelm III as a place of higher learning. HU was originally called Berlin University, and went through several different titles before being renamed in 1949 to honor the founder Wilhelm von Humboldt, a renowned Prussian educator and linguist, and his younger brother Alexander von Humboldt, an equally celebrated explorer, geographer, and naturalist. Humboldt's vision was of a university that would unite both teaching and research to offer students access to the best all-around thinkers of their age—as well as the opportunity to join their ranks. HU was one of eleven in Germany to be named "University of Excellence" in 2012. Fitting, since it acted as a model for many of the best universities offering liberal arts educations today—truly the "mother of all modern universities." as Humboldt himself claimed.

In addition to offering degrees in law and medicine, HU also covers all major academic disciplines: arts and humanities (including philosophy, history, literature, and languages), social and cultural science, natural sciences, mathematics, agriculture, and theology. Numerous study courses in pursuit of translation, interpretation, and teaching qualifications are also offered, and the university has even seen fit to adapt its curricula to new fields of study reflecting evolving 21st century interests, such as gender studies. The newest campus in Adlershof in Berlin's southeast opened in 2003; it is specifically for the study of science and industry and the development of new technology and information services.

Most of the 20th century, from the rise of the Third Reich to the fall of the Berlin Wall, proved to be tumultuous for the HU. After seeing a large part of its faculty either fired and stripped of their degrees or arrested and deported under the Nazis, the university was also unlucky enough to be on the wrong side of the post-war division: in the east. When it became clear that communist influence had severely changed the university in both structure and content, students and faculty broke out in protest. The result was an ideological split, leading to the founding of a new university in 1948, the **Freie Universität** (literally "free university") in Dahlem. Once the Wall was built in 1961, it was clear that the split would last. Over the years, the

Freie Universität or FU cemented its status as a top university, and still ranks among the best in Germany.

FU was founded under the auspices of not only West Berlin politicians, but also American allied forces, since Dahlem was located in the American sector. Generous donations from the United States funded the building efforts in the late '40s and early '50s, and even today the campus somehow feels distinctly American—much like the leafy suburban college towns surrounding institutions of higher learning in the US. From the start, FU, much like West Berlin at the time, had to work doubly hard to attract students. The fact that it managed to do so was also due to a great deal of international support, and today FU still feels like the more international, open, and in many ways less formal of the two universities.

In addition to medicine (including dentistry and veterinary medicine) and law, FU also offers courses of study in the humanities (philosophy, language, literature, history, art history, anthropology and cultural studies), sciences (physics, biology, chemistry, psychology, pharmacology, earth science, and meteorology), political science, mathematics and computer science, and theology. In keeping with its origins, it has a John F. Kennedy Institute for North American Studies along with institutes for Eastern European and Latin American studies. There are also a fair number of study programs conducted entirely in English for which no proof of German is necessary, including international health, international relations, gender studies, and a number of medical, scientific, and literary fields.

Charité is the medical school for both HU and FU. It has several campuses in Berlin, and is one of the largest and oldest teaching hospitals in Europe, with a history spanning 300 years. In addition to boasting a great number of Nobel prizewinners, Charité was also home to some of the last century's greatest medical discoveries and advancements. In addition to a number of worldwide collaborations and partner organizations, Charité also offers a continuing education program in English and German for healthcare professionals at its International Academy.

The union of several academic institutions over a period of more than a century resulted in the creation of Berlin's **Technische Universität** (TU) or University of Technology. Not only was the TU one of the first institutions to promote engineering during the industrial revolution of the 19th century, it was also the first technical school to be given the right to grant doctorates by Kaiser Wilhelm II in 1899. Its sprawling campus on Charlottenburg's Ernst-Reuter-Platz boasts a sprinkling of grand Prussian edifices along with more modern buildings. Unsurprisingly the departments or "faculties" within the TU focus strongly on science and engineering. They include mathematics and natural sciences, electrical engineering and computer science, transport and mechanical systems, planning, building and environment, process sciences, and economics and management. It perhaps may seem strange, but the TU also offers a program in the humanities or *Geisteswissenschaften*, focusing less on traditional liberal arts subjects and more on how culture, human thought, and human development have led to the discovery and advancement of scientific subjects. The humanities include a center for feminist and gender studies, an institute of speech and communication, and a center for "metropolitan" or urban studies.

The **Universität der Künste** (UdK) or University of the Arts used to be called the Hochschule der Künste until 2001—a significant name change since, as you may remember, *Hochschule* is a college or trade school, whereas *Universität* is closer to the English concept of the university—an establishment for higher learning. UdK is one of Germany's few art institutions with full university status, including the right to award doctorates. It offers courses of study in four colleges—fine arts, music, performing arts, and architecture, media, and design—as well as what it calls inter-disciplinary centers—the Jazz Institute of Berlin (JIB) where UdK students collaborate with those from Berlin's **Hochschule für Musik Hanns Eisler (Academy of Music)**, and the Center for Dance (HZT), a collaboration with the **Hochschule für Schauspielkunst Ernst Busch (Academy of Dramatic Art)** and Berlin dance professionals in cooperation with Tanzraum Berlin. UdK has multiple school buildings across the west, and a modern university library right beside Zoo station. Students can choose courses that culminate in a BA, MA, or Doctorate, and can focus solely on artistic training or add pedagogical training, which gives them an opportunity to teach in their own artistic fields. Another art academy besides Hanns Eisler and Ernst Busch is the **Kunsthochschule Weißensee**.

The public schools (including all four universities) receive government money to operate and therefore charge little to no tuition, only asking that their students pay certain fees and contributions. FU's website, for example lists its extra charges as a registration fee, contributions to the student union and government, and the **BVG *Semesterticket***. (Of course, this all adds up to less than 300 Euros.) Be aware, however, that you should still have some savings or a semi-regular income to support yourself. According to the FU website, in order to obtain a student visa at the *Ausländerbehörde*, non-EU students have to show that they have 600-700 Euros available for monthly expenses, outside of income they may earn from a student job.

Aside from the four main universities, there are multiple colleges, academies, and specialty schools offering a top education in a number of fields. **Private business schools** include the Business School Berlin Potsdam (BSP) and the European School of Management and Technology (ESMT). The Hertie School of Governance is an international, private university offering programs in public policy and governance for students who have backgrounds in law, economics, or international relations. Its classes are taught entirely in English.

APPLYING

As a non-German applying to school in Berlin, you will find the application procedure more streamlined than that of many comparable international universities and also—at least for you—a lot more complicated. Not only you will have to provide most of your documentation in German (time to hire an accredited translator), you will also be in the unenviable position of having to figure out how your non-German background and qualifications fit into the German system. It was already pretty difficult in the past to determine whether your foreign Bachelor's degree was enough to get you into a Master's program in Berlin. Now it's even more so, as the entire BA/MA degree system underwent a recent overhaul in response to the so-called **Bologna Process** in 1999, which aimed to standardize the education system Europe-wide. (Such a system would mean that an Italian student, for example, would have a much easier time studying in Germany, as the educational framework and number of required credits would be the same in both countries.)

If you studied outside the EU, you may find it difficult to present yourself as a worthy candidate for a Master's or Doctorate in Germany when your Bachelor's comes from another continent. Furthermore, many schools have introduced dual BA/MA-track programs, making it impossible to slip into the Master's program halfway, meaning that some students who come to Germany with Bachelor's qualifications wishing to study for a Master's face the prospect of having to study for a Bachelor's all over again. Of course, this is not the case at all schools, and the international programs at the four universities usually allow for a bit of wiggle room, as long as prospective students don't try to apply for a Master's in a field that has nothing to do with their Bachelor's. In Germany the two are often considered a whole, with the Master's seen as a natural progression of the Bachelor's, allowing a student to delve even more deeply into a subject.

That being said, if you plan on applying to HU, FU, or TU, Uni-Assist will become your best friend. Founded specifically to aid international students wishing to study in Germany, **Uni-Assist** is an application service designed to streamline the process. You will need copies of previous certificates of study translated into German (both copies and translations must bear a stamp and signature of authentication), as well as sufficient proof of German, unless your study course will be in English. As forms of proof, universities will accept either the DSH (Deutsche Sprachprüfung für den Hochschulzugang or German Language Examination for College Entry) or the TestDaF (Deutsch als Fremdsprache or German as a Foreign Language Test). Sometimes it is enough to submit a certificate of completion of a C2 level course at the Goethe-Institut. A standard application form can be found on the Uni-Assist website, and then either printed, filled out and sent via post, or submitted online. Some universities have special application forms they would rather you use, so it is important to check the requirements of each school. Fill out one copy of the application form for each school you apply to.

Acceptance rates are based on what's called the **Numerus Clausus** or limited admissions policy. Since public universities do not have minimum grading criteria by which to accept students, they instead set limits on how many places are available in each subject. Whether or not you will be accepted certainly depends on how good a student you were, but only in relation to the other applicants competing with you for places. Moreover, there are specific quotas within a course of study, so international applicants will not be competing with Germans for spaces, but only with each other. Uni-Assist stores your documents for one year in its archives, giving you the chance to apply again if you didn't make it the first time around.

For arts schools like the UdK, admission is far more subjective. In addition to a certificate of study completion from your home country and proof of German, you will of course have to submit a CV detailing your accomplishments and artistic background, as well as sample materials. In the case of music or performing arts, dates are set for the applicant to be tested in musical theory and to perform a range of pieces. In the case of fine arts, architecture, and design, a portfolio is required. Some disciplines also require the successful completion of a task or assignment within a set period of time, demonstrating how well students can improvise and think on their feet. Each specific field of study within the UdK has its own entrance criteria, and its own webpage with information in German and English.

STUDENT HOUSING

Student housing isn't such a big thing in Berlin. That's partially because finding a room in Berlin has always been fairly easy and cheap, but also due to the German or European point of view that students are adults and should be treated as such. Studentenwerk runs residential halls called **Wohnheime**, including one student hotel (Studentenhotel Hubertusallee) that rents to Berlin students during the school semester and visiting students over the summer. The Max-Kade-Haus on Theodor-Heuss-Platz is reserved exclusively for international students. Thirty-six residential halls can be found in every Berlin district, housing up to 9,500 students per year. Room prices are roughly the same or a bit less than in a shared apartment (up to 300 Euros a month), although some halls rent out rooms by the night for students who may be looking for their own places, but need somewhere to crash in the meantime. Sometimes Studentenwerk also offers students package deals that include a room in a residential hall, a certain number of meal vouchers, and student health insurance.

University notice boards (*Schwarzes Brett*—literally "black-board") can also prove fertile ground for apartment vacancies: very often students or faculty will post, looking for a *Nachmieter* to take over their space when they leave. Start trolling early, however; once classes start and everyone has settled in, it will be a lot more difficult to find places opening up mid-semester. (See Chapter 4: Finding a Place to Live)

STUDENT JOBS

In general, university students are meant to spend most of their time studying, and are usually given a limit on how many semesters they can spend working towards a single degree in order to deter them from taking on more than they can handle. What's more, students are generally expected to have enough money to support themselves while studying without taking on a job (no word on how they do this, though). Nevertheless, most students elect to take on at least part-time work to help pay the bills and finance leisure activities.

Student jobs are permitted in most cases but well regulated to keep them from becoming the main focus of a student's life. These regulations depend largely on what country a student is from, how much money he or she makes, or how many hours the job takes. EU citizens are allowed to work as much as they want, although as soon as they start making more than 450 Euros, they have to pay taxes and pay into social security. Non-EU citizens are given a separate stipulation as part of their student visa: 120 full days (eight-hour days) or 240 half days (four-hour days) per year. Any more and you will need to obtain permission from the *Ausländerbehörde*.

Also be aware that the student jobs you may find cannot be freelance positions, as freelancing is expressly forbidden on a student visa (just as studying is forbidden on a freelance visa). This means you will have a set monthly salary paid by an employer, and a set number of hours or shifts you are expected to work. Finding a job in connection with your university (as a teaching assistant, for example, or in the library) can be your easiest bet. Internships are also permitted, but be forewarned: any internship, even an unpaid one, unfairly enough, will eat into your 120-day work limit unless it is required as part of your program of study. Students receiving any kind of funding, including grants, are normally not allowed to work alongside their studies.

Many universities have job centers or online job boards of their own, but sometimes it pays to make the rounds, visiting bars and restaurants in your neighborhood, or seeing if local shops or supermarkets are hiring. These jobs are not meant to be yours forever; they're only meant to support you until you graduate.

WORK LIFE IN BERLIN

You probably already know that Berlin suffers from high unemployment despite being the capital of the EU's top earner. This has nothing to do with Berliners' general intelligence quotient or ability to work (although some Germans from the wealthier parts of the country might disagree on that). Rather, Berlin seems to have been struck by bad fortune repeatedly over the last century, keeping it isolated in many ways. After being ravaged by the effects of two wars, Berlin was abandoned by many of its moneymakers. This left its remaining residents with something of a paradox, simultaneously living in a strategically important city yet feeling left behind as the rest of the West surged ahead. Even today, many Germans still seem to take little notice of Berlin simply because it is considered so inferior to economic powerhouses like Munich or Stuttgart. Berlin may be touted as Europe's most exciting city, but some Germans continue to see it as the rather irritating younger sibling still trying to catch up.

Slowly but surely, things are improving. The Berlin bug is starting to catch on among once-reluctant industries as well as ambitious newcomers. Companies are starting to trickle back in again, while the few that never left are getting swept along by the rising tide of Berlin mania and set to grow even more. Nowadays, even tech companies based in Silicon Valley or New York are considering opening branches here. The future is looking bright; at least for those connected and educated enough to find jobs. Berlin's unemployed population consists largely of immigrants who do not speak the language or former East Germans who still trail their West German counterparts in terms of education, employment, and the number of high-ranking government or cultural positions they've managed to reach. For these people the uphill climb is steeper, and one can only hope that Berlin will find space for them amidst its explosive growth instead of leaving them behind.

Then again, perhaps Berlin's destiny is not to be like its older siblings at all, but rather to forge a path as a new kind of 21st century city where industry is a presence but does not rule, and where creativity matters far more than straight-up capitalism. As one of Berlin's newest residents, you have an opportunity to be part of that change, to have a hand in the shaping of Berlin's future. In the meantime, of course, you still need to eat and pay your rent.

THE CV OR *LEBENSLAUF*

Unless you arrive in Berlin speaking perfect German, you probably won't be going through the normal channels to find work. That being said, knowing what to expect when you arrive can go a long way towards tempering your expectations and giving you the adequate tools to prepare for the job search. There is a certain know-how required to navigate the German job market, which even those who live in Germany might not fully grasp before making a few mistakes. As a foreigner, learning how to present yourself as a job candidate in Germany is only half the battle; the other half is learning how to present yourself so well, you'll convince the person interviewing you that you could do an even better job than a German.

Even if you come here with work permission and a fine grasp of German, the first thing you will need to do is craft a perfect resumé or CV, called a *Lebenslauf.* In keeping with the German propensity for organization and clarity, Germans used to expect a *Lebenslauf* to be in chronological order, with education at the top, followed by first jobs and ending with your most recent one. This has changed recently, however, and it is now acceptable to arrange work history and education in reverse chronological order, with your most recent job at the top. Furthermore, although this may seem wildly counterintuitive to putting up a professional front, Germans think nothing of adding personal details like age, address, marriage status and even hobbies to a *Lebenslauf.* You may also have heard that Germans expect every *Lebenslauf* to come with a photo—at best a professional looking one. It's hard to argue with those who claim this is discriminatory—in fact, German companies are not allowed to demand that job applications include a photo. All the same, applications that do not are often intentionally or unintentionally disregarded, making for a real Catch 22. Some maintain that, although the inclusion of a photo might encourage or aid discriminatory practices, a German of Turkish descent is just as likely to have a Turkish name as to look Turkish in a photo, and will therefore have just as much of a hurdle to overcome when it comes to applying for jobs. The application process cannot be completely blind, the argument goes, and keeping your name off your CV is simply not an option. Most German companies would still prefer the option to put a face to a name. Hence, a photo is still necessary.

FREELANCE WORK

In most European capitals these days, you'll barely be able to make ends meet unless you have a full-time job, and a well-paid one at that. Not so in Berlin, where it often seems that half the populace is barely working by choice, and the other half is engaged in some kind of artistic pursuit that hardly counts as a job. While things may change in the next decade, right now Berlin is still cheap enough that you don't have to work fulltime to be able to afford a decent living standard. If you want to join the ranks of the working, freelance, part-time, or full-time, there are a few things you should know.

Finding freelance work, not just in Berlin but anywhere, is very often a matter of creating it yourself. Sometimes there will be job listings to peruse, but they very often won't fit the parameters you've envisioned for yourself. Finding freelance work is less a matter of sending out a full German *Lebenslauf* and more a matter of finding a way into a company through the back door: figuring out how best to approach a company about the work you think they need done, and how to present yourself as the best person to do it.

Many freelancers get their start by offering services in their own language. While this may work if you come from a country with a robust market in which Germany takes an interest, it can actually end up being pretty useless by this point if your native language is English, as there are simply so many English speakers running around Berlin, all looking for jobs. All the same, if your German is good enough to **translate**, approaching companies who may want to have more of an international presence might serve you well. Furthermore, there are endless numbers of Berliners, both students and professionals, who must write something official in English, be it a paper or office report, and simply need a native speaker to make sure it sounds perfect. Whether you'll be the first native speaker to appear when they need one is sort of a matter of luck, but you can up your chances by sending out word to all your contacts that you're looking for work. You can also post messages advertising your services either online or on message boards in university buildings. As with most jobs, once you've successfully corrected a student's fifty-page thesis, he's bound to have friends who will also need help.

Other new Berliners hope to get jobs **teaching English**, either privately or with a school. True, the choice of English schools in Berlin can seem endless, but so can the number of hopefuls applying to teach English every year. You're unlikely to get anywhere without a certificate from an accredited school for teaching English as a second language, like the CELTA (Certificate in English Language Teaching to Adults) awarded by Cambridge University. Even if you have this, however, it's only the beginning. Expect competition to be fierce, and use all your resources to advertise yourself, find private clients, and get in touch with schools that may have openings now or later. Don't rule out the old-fashioned way: sometimes going by foot from school to school, dropping off CVs and introducing yourself, is the best way to get to know them and give them the chance to get to know you.

If your expertise is in **coding, social media, or PR**, expect to have a slightly easier time, as virtually every new company in Berlin needs one or all of these. It doesn't take long to put together a list of new startups in town, as most of them like to make it quite public that they've made a home in Berlin. If you want to get in on this scene but have no idea where to start, a lot of startups sponsor regular events that are the perfect opportunity for networking. Sign up for their newsletters and keep track of what's going on. The best way to get hired is to know and make friends with the people who might need to hire somebody. Also, since many of them are international and speak English already, you get the added bonus of not having to learn German before taking the plunge. **Venture Village** (www. venturevillage.eu) is a good place to stay informed, as they offer a weekly newsletter covering the tech and startup scene that anyone can sign up for. They also have a blog offering pretty entertaining commentary about what it's like to be a foreigner in Berlin.

If you can afford it on a freelancer's salary, try to get a desk at a **co-working space**. These are popping up all over town and, much like the Factory, are also spaces for half work, half play, where freelancers can come together to network, support each other, give valuable feedback, and occasionally hunker down and work. Co-working spaces run the gamut from serious and quiet (for those who don't want any distractions) to something like a Berlin version of a college dorm—a place where you go to interact with people around you. Freelancing at home can be ideal for some, but for others it is downright lonely, and can become a dead end. Since so much about finding freelance work is connecting with real people in real time, you may simply want to put yourself in a situation where you're forced to do so. That way, even if you're staring into a computer screen eight hours a day to make a deadline, you'll still have real live humans in the room, ready to strike up a conversation or offer help and support if you look desperate. Who knows? One of them may even lead you to your next job. Some co-working spaces in Berlin:

- **Betahaus** is a multi-level space just off of Moritzplatz that also hosts events.
- **Agora Collective** in Neukölln has an in-house café and hosts meet-ups, workshops, and events.
- **Ahoy!** in Charlottenburg is a beautiful loft space that's more like a clubhouse.
- **Cluboffice** is a network of upscale and professional shared office spaces.

FULL-TIME WORK

Finding full-time work in Berlin is not easy. If you're coming here as a non-EU citizen with very little knowledge of German, your chances of getting hired are extremely slim. That being said, the explosion of Berlin-based startups has provided at least a short-term solution. The only question is whether these startups are here to stay, or whether half of them will drop out once the going gets tough and the competition tougher.

If you do have permission to work in Germany and a decent grasp of the language, then start doing some serious networking. If a certain company catches your eye, try to find out as much as possible about it before making first contact. Ideally, you have a connection you can milk for some kind of advice about how best to frame your approach. You don't have to show tremendous excitement or enthusiasm for a potential job in your cover letter or in person—in fact, some German companies may be taken aback by such overt displays of affection—but you should at least feel some.

Once a company has expressed interest in hiring you, expect to go through a long-winded vetting process that will include not just interviews, but also a trial period of six months, called a **Probezeit**. Go about it with the expectation that you may be hired freelance long before a company considers taking you on full-time. Berlin's dirty little secret is perhaps that many freelancers merely fall into that lifestyle instead of choosing it. Indeed, many would rather enjoy the security of a full-time job and were once looking for one, but then got discouraged and took whatever they could get. There simply aren't enough to go around, and companies that do offer full-time positions often put their potential employees through the ringer, making them start off as interns and then go through years of limited, one- or two-year contracts that must constantly be renewed, their job performance almost always up for review. Your first full-time contract may only be for a year. Your second contract may only be for two years. Germany's labor laws, just like Germany's real estate laws, make it very difficult to kick someone out. If you're lucky enough to get a fulltime, unlimited contract, you're pretty much in for life, so the company hiring you wants to make sure you'll never become a liability.

You may be used to considering annual **salaries** in your home country, but in Germany, contracts are usually presented with the salary quoted per month. When assessing an offer, keep in mind that the figure quoted will be before taxes and benefits, meaning you'll need to subtract a percentage of it depending on your tax status or *Steuerklasse* to get an idea of your take-home pay. (The handy tax calculator at www.brutto-netto-rechner.org will also show you how much employers must pay into the system for each employee, including you.) Once you're in, though, you'll be pleasantly surprised by the comfort and assurance it provides. In Germany, full-time work always comes "with benefits", so your employer will pay half your health insurance and contribute to your pension.

You usually won't be given an allotment of **sick days**, but rather can take them whenever you need them, as long as you are *krankgeschrieben* or "written in sick," which means you've gone to a doctor who has checked out your symptoms and written you a note declaring you officially sick. Employees are usually allowed one or even three days off without a note (how else would they have time to get one?) and are then required to present something official if they want more time. Parents have the option of taking a certain number of days to care for sick children.

^ *No ordinary day job: cooking at the Markthalle IX in Kreuzberg*

You'll have about four to six weeks of **vacation**, depending on the industry. You are free to take them when you wish, and yearly holidays are usually not included. What's more, unlike in America, where workers are made to feel guilty for every minute not spent at the office, in Germany you'll be met with cheer when you decide to take your annual holidays. You will not be expected to work half days while you're away, nor will you be expected to be in constant contact with the office. In Germany, vacation is as sacred as lunch hour: a time to recharge, enjoy life, and come back to the office refreshed and ready to work again.

Speaking of **lunch hour**, many big companies in Germany provide their workers with subsidized lunches at their very own *Kantine* (cafeteria), which you'll probably get roped into visiting whether you want to or not. Try to take advantage of it: while *Kantine* food is hardly something to get excited about, *Kantine* culture is a crucial part of the German work environment; a time when colleagues can sit together and talk about something other than work, building crucial friendships and partnerships that can grow both in and beyond the office. Try to spend at least a half hour with your fellow workers, commiserating about such and such and reviewing what you did on your vacations. (Bonus: if you're just beginning to learn German, this is a perfect time to practice!) If your company does not have a *Kantine*, you will of course be given a lunch hour. Be aware of what your company considers lunch hour, though: some are pretty stingy, requiring you to work exactly eight hours not including lunch, in which case a longer lunch break means you'll have to stay later to make up the time. Some companies can also be strict about when you take your lunch break just because they consider it crucial that someone be there to man the desks and answer phones at all times: don't be surprised if you have to have a daily conversation with your co-workers about who is eating when.

Again, depending on the industry, you may find German work life to be pleasantly laid back or extremely formal. Startup culture is known as exactly that (a "culture") because of startups' casual attitudes towards work versus play. Many startup offices have gaming rooms, pizza parties, and beer readily available, as the entire point is to provide workers with an ersatz family and a pseudo friendship circle as well as the environment they need to be creative and productive. Old-school German companies and especially government and academic offices can be quite strict in their codes of conduct, with employees addressing each other with the formal "Sie" instead of the informal "Du," even if they've been working together for years. Like many things in Europe, however, this kind of emphasis on formality is slowly eroding to make way for a more Americanized version of office culture that sits somewhere between these two extremes; a place where employees can be a slightly better, more refined, more polite version of themselves.

INTERNSHIPS

Many starry-eyed new Berliners arrive in the city expecting to find work and instead find themselves falling into the internship trap. The traditional German internship or *Praktikum* comes with a salary of not more than 450 Euros per month, as this is the amount a company can legally pay for a full-time intern without paying many of the taxes that would go along with a real salary. If you're lucky, the company may go the official route and pay into your pension plan as well, but it is by no means required to. Of course, not all internships are created equal, and some offer more legitimate job tracks than others, but it can be hard to know the difference. Whether they're talking about internships that lead to actual careers or merely six months of unpaid labor, most Germans agree that there are far too many of them, leading to a situation deemed **Generation Praktikum** (Generation Internship): an entire generation of young people in Germany stuck in an endless loop of non-paid or low-paid work. Indeed, while internships are not uniformly exploitative or even uniformly bad, there are a lot of companies that will take advantage of an endless supply of desperate young people by taking on interns year after year, actually hiring less than one percent of them full-time at the end.

How to be sure what you're getting yourself into? Well, first of all, check the company's history and credentials. If you're about to start a six-month internship at a company with very few actual employees but five times as many interns, then that gives you a pretty good idea of whether or not they will ask you to stick around after your internship. The fact that these companies have plenty of work to be done but not enough money to pay their employees certainly says something about their business practices, and how successful they will probably be in the future. Be wary, too, of overly earnest new companies, especially startups, looking for unpaid workers: they may not call what you're doing an internship, but you'll nevertheless be part of a team working for free in hopes of creating a product good enough to secure investment capital. Occasionally, these sorts of ventures pay off, but for every startup that receives millions in investment funding, another hundred drop off the face of the earth, dropping you back into the job market.

If you do want to gain valuable experience and contacts through an internship, your best bet is probably a company that has a real internship program. These are often older, well-established companies that are truly interested in taking on interns in order to train them for the industry, not just because they can't afford to pay real employees. These companies are likely to have internships for short, set periods of time, offering interns a good deal of variation in their tasks around a department or in several departments. They are also more likely to be concerned that an intern is actually learning something, and to have a certain person tasked with overseeing the program. True, these companies are not often the most exciting or innovative ones, but they offer some reliability and oversight that can be hard to find in Berlin's hectic and ill-regulated fashion, PR, and startup industries.

Some companies offer internships in conjunction with an academic degree or trade school program, called an *Ausbildung*. These are often quite well regulated, as they are usually required for school credit and hence must fit certain criteria. A company is also much more likely to accept these students as interns, since they are already studying to obtain a degree in the industry. They might even have some prior experience, so they won't require as much training. It is these internships that are most likely to lead to a job offer in the end; if not at the actual company, then at least in the same field.

Make no mistake about it, though; interns are at the bottom rung of the ladder, and they're usually made to feel that way. If you've just arrived in Berlin after university, you may think you're too old for an internship. Well, welcome to *Generation Praktikum*, where many Germans end up interning well into their twenties or even thirties. If you think you can do better than an internship, you probably can, but that doesn't mean starting off with one will be a complete waste of time: just take care you aren't exploited simply because you don't know what's fair, or what is expected of the average intern in Berlin. Conversely, an internship may be a good, low-pressure way for you to learn the ropes of an industry here, and to make friends when you first arrive.

You may have also heard the term **Minijob**. These are like internships but even less beneficial: whereas an internship ideally offers young people a foot in the door to their industry of choice, a *Minijob* is just another name for a low-wage, low-skilled job (with few work hours). Introduced in 2003 by former chancellor Gerhard Schröder, the minijob allows employees of any age to earn 450 Euros a month without paying taxes. It hardly needs to be pointed out that this is a tough sum to live on, but still, some do. Recent criticism of this concept has been tied to the debate over the minimum wage (which Germany will institute for the first time in 2015) and a general malaise over the widening gap between rich and poor, even in such an economically successful country.

STARTUP HYPE

For all the excitement surrounding the startup scene, startups are only as good as the products they sell, and will only last as long as those products are popular. In Internet years, that may not be very long. If you do end up getting a job with one of them, best to keep a level head. Berlin startup hype is much like Berlin hype in general: it can sweep you up if you're not careful, making you believe that what you're selling or the company you're working for is of utmost importance in the world. Most companies, just like most cities, succeed as a result of a foundation myth. Startups are no different, only sometimes the myth is all you have, as the company has neither received many rounds of investment capital nor succeeded in making a profit of its own.

Some of Berlin's most successful and best-known startups:
- **Zalando,** which has copied the US company Zappos as an online retailer selling clothing and shoes from different brands directly to consumers
- **Wimdu**, which allows travelers to rent private homes while opening up their own for rental, much like the worldwide apartment sharing service **Airbnb**
- **Soundcloud**, an online platform for the uploading, distribution, and sharing of user-generated audio
- **Kitchensurfing,** which offers a profile platform for chefs to advertise their cooking and catering services or promote private supper clubs

In some ways, Berlin was always ripe for the startup takeover. In a city where the lack of industry had left a big, gaping hole in the economy, it was perhaps only natural that the first companies to see Berlin's potential again would be part of the new Internet-based economy, able to transcend a lot of what made traditional industries stagnate post-war. Most of Berlin's startups are breeding grounds for young, creative, and international misfits—the types of people Berlin has always attracted. Startups are an extremely powerful asset to a city like Berlin, something even chancellor Angela Merkel has acknowledged by publicly pledging support for this economy of the future. If you feel it could be your future as well, there's no better time to get in on the startup scene—with realistic expectations, of course.

TAXES

If you've ever been employed in your own country, this won't come as a much of a shock: Germany expects you to pay taxes. How much, how often, and of what sort will depend a lot on how you make a living. If you are a full-time employee, you are eligible for what's called a *Lohnsteuerkarte* or Tax ID card, which helps your employer keep track of how much tax to deduct. The paper card traditionally recorded details of your tax class and any life circumstances that allowed for deductions. The *Lohnsteuerkarte* system has now gone entirely online, and can be accessed using your birthdate and *Identifikationsnummer*, a unique ID number assigned to each person working in Germany.

Of course, while Germans are now assigned an **ID number** automatically from birth, those moving to Germany from elsewhere must go through the fairly painless process of obtaining one at the *Finanzamt*: you'll need your passport and registration (*Meldebescheinigung*) and will be asked for essential information like name, address, marital status, and oddly enough, religion. This determines whether you owe taxes to the Protestant or Catholic church of Germany. (If you're not German, you probably won't want to pay 9% of your income to either one, and must therefore declare yourself church-free. If you do accidentally register yourself with a church, be aware that correcting the mistake is possible, but can take a lot of time and paperwork.) All this will determine your *Steuerklasse* ("tax class"), which is really a bit of a misnomer. It has nothing to do with how much money you make and everything to do with your marital and parental status. If you're single, you're class I. If you're a single parent, you're class II. If you're married and make more than your spouse, you are class III and your spouse class V. Class IV is reserved for both halves of a married couple with nearly equal incomes. Class VI is only for those who have a second job outside of their main income provider.

If wish to work as a freelancer in Germany, you will still need to obtain a **Steuernummer** from the *Finanzamt*. Once you obtain this number, you will need to print it on every invoice you write, as well as label your tax forms with it when you declare your income. If you forget to label an invoice with your *Steuernummer*, it should under no circumstances be paid, lest it by considered illegal (*Schwarz* or "black") money. Keep in mind that, although you may see the *Steuernummer* as a kind of ID number as well, it is not the same as your *Identifikationsnummer*. Your ID number identifies you as an individual, regardless of your work situation or what companies you have founded or are affiliated with (a person starting a company needs a different number than a person simply working freelance). You may have different *Steuernummern* over a lifetime, but your *Identifikationsnummer* stays with you. If you are working as a freelancer, you may also want to apply for what's called an **Umsatzsteuernummer**. As opposed to the normal Steuernummer, which only functions in Germany, the *Umsatzsteuernummer* or USt-ID-Nr. for short is recognized and valid EU-wide.

To complicate things even further, when you go into the Finanzamt to declare yourself a freelancer and get your *Steuernummer*, you should have a pretty good idea of how much money you expect to make in the coming year. For those just starting out in Germany, this should not be too hard: you will probably make very little money your first year here. Of course, knowing you'll make "very little" is not the same as having an exact estimate, but this is what you'll need to label yourself a **Kleinunternehmer**, one of Germany's small gifts to freelancers. If you declare yourself a Kleinunternehmer or small enterprise, it means you expect to make 17,500 Euros or less this year (the exact amount often changes, so make sure to ask someone at the *Finanzamt*). As a *Kleinunternehmer*, you technically do not have to pay taxes at all. You can write invoices without adding *Mehrwertsteuer* or VAT, and do not have to keep track of this to pay to the government at year's end. You may also file your taxes yearly instead of quarterly or even monthly, as some high-earning freelancers are required to, depending on how much money you make. Even as a *Kleinunternehmer*, it is good to keep track of all your expenses and invoices, and to make a report that you can submit with your tax return at the end of the year, summing up how much you spent and how much you made. This will give you a good overview of how well you're doing financially every year—an important thing to keep track of as a freelancer, regardless of your income.

If you expect to make more than the *Kleinunternehmer* limit, you must also write this on your tax number application. You will be given both a *Steuernummer* and an *Umsatzsteuernummer* and must not only file your taxes more regularly, but also pay taxes owed in advance of filing. Of course, any expenses that go towards your business can be used to lessen your tax burden, so if you travel a lot for work or pay for a website redesign, make sure you save all your bills.

It can be a major annoyance for freelancers to have to pay taxes this way, and quite a headache to remember all the exceptions and deductions long enough to apply them. This is why many freelancers (including doctors and lawyers, who are also considered freelance if they have their own practice) employ a **Steuerberater** or tax advisor. In fact, many fulltime employees also use them, just because the German tax code is so dauntingly complex, it takes an expert to figure it out. Tax advisors charge a fee of anywhere between one hundred and several hundred Euros, depending on the complexity of the tasks required, but usually end up saving you more money than you spend. If you're a foreign freelancer earning money with multiple clients in both your home country and Germany, finding a *Steuerberater* who is familiar with both tax codes is all the more crucial.

UNEMPLOYMENT

If you have lost your job, you may be eligible for **Arbeitslosengeld** that takes into account your former salary and how much you paid into the system. If you are unable to find a job in the first place, or have been out of work for so long that you officially join the ranks of the long-term unemployed, you may be eligible for Hartz IV or social welfare, which was reformed in 2005. Under the new system, *Arbeitslosengeld* is known as Unemployment Benefit I and Hartz IV, which is known as Unemployment Benefit II, kicks in once your time on *Arbeitslosengeld* has run out.

In order to be eligible for *Arbeitslosengeld* in Germany, you must have had a full-time job at some point, usually for at least twelfe months, when some of your pay was deducted and deposited into an unemployment fund. In order to receive benefits, you must register yourself with the *Arbeitsamt* or employment office as being out of work but in search of a job. You must do this as soon as you know you're losing your job to allow the *Arbeitsamt* time to process your claim so that the benefits will kick in by your last workday. Technically, if you are unemployed and have no children, you are entitled to 60 percent of your former pay for up to 24 months, depending on your age and how long you paid into the system.

If you have worked fulltime in Germany but now wish to start a new life as a freelancer, a little-known option may also be available to you: instead of simply registering for *Arbeitslosengeld*, you can register for an **Existenzgründung**, declaring your desire to set up your own business or reinvent yourself as a freelancer. You'll have to prove competence in the field you hope to go into, while also convincing the authorities that your quality of life will be higher as a freelancer than a full-time employee, and that you have a legitimate reason, be it financial or psychological, for wanting to make a living on your own. The support you get can be truly beneficial, giving you the time and money you need to launch your business while also allowing you the opportunity to take state-sponsored courses on entrepreneurship, get valuable advice from industry professionals, and—best of all—continue unemployment benefits even when your first jobs start rolling in.

The dreaded **Hartz IV** has been the subject of much debate over the years, and in spite of all the German government's tinkering, it has not yet been perfected (if such a thing is possible). The number IV refers to the fourth in a collection of reforms put in place in 2005 in an attempt to overturn the job market and reinvent it for a new era, in the words of former chancellor Gerhard Schröder of the Social Democratic Party (SPD). Whereas previously, those seeking unemployment benefits had to apply separately, at multiple offices, for various sums of money, Hartz IV united them all under one roof, making administration and oversight more efficient. In order to be eligible for Hartz IV, you must not only be out of work, you must also lack an income that comes close to supporting your needs. You also have to demonstrate a desire to find work, which often means taking whatever meager job may be thrown at you by the *Arbeitsamt*, which not only processes unemployment benefits but also finds the unemployed new work. In a much-debated part of these reforms, the government began offering what are known as **Ein-Euro-Jobs** to Hartz IV recipients in an effort to get them out of their homes and back into the workforce. While these jobs are meant to show one's ability to work and supplement one's Hartz IV earnings, they are not meant to replace real employment (at 1-3 Euros per hour, they pay too little).

In many German cities, workers may have been driven to get off Hartz IV and get back into the job market by the high cost of living. Of course, a better economy and better industrial infrastructure mean more jobs are available in the first place to those who need them. In Berlin, however, living on Hartz IV has been a real possibility for a long time, and still is today in certain areas. German benefits are by no means expansive, but they are still pretty generous in comparison to many EU countries.

They might be loathe to say it in public, as it proves all the old clichés about German nationalism, but many Germans will admit in private that they think the system is far too beneficial to those who didn't pay in, and should be overhauled yet again. Their opinion is that a system designed solely for the benefit of German citizens, EU citizens, and others who have legal working status in Germany would be more efficient and fair. In a few years, partially as a result of the continued repercussions of the 2008 financial crisis, an overhaul may indeed come. Critics of Hartz IV argue that it has led to greater unemployment, although in fact it has really only created more claimants by widening the circumstances under which one may claim. Other vocal opponents of Hartz IV argue that it doesn't do enough for the unemployed. It may be too early to say whether the reforms are here to stay, or whether the critics of Germany's current social welfare standards will be loud enough to effect real change. For your own purposes, unemployment should be viewed as a last resort you're lucky to have, rather than a cushion to lie back and get comfortable on.

SHOPPING, COOKING, AND EATING

140 While Berlin's food situation has improved in the last decade, it still has a long way to go when compared with other European capitals. Still, Germany should not be entirely faulted for this—especially northern Germany. It's hard to know what to do with fresh fruits and vegetables in a country that grows relatively few of its own. Many older Germans will have one or two classic dishes up their sleeves, to be brought out at a lavish Christmas meal or to impress dinner guests. These dishes will almost always consist of meat (usually pork but sometimes beef) cooked in one of several ways, depending on the region, accompanied by potatoes, noodles, boiled vegetables, or a combination of the three.

There has long been a maddening lack of options at city supermarkets, but some Berliners (yes, many of them international, and many of them well-to-do) are starting to expect and demand better. A sizable part of the Prenzlauer Berg population, for example, would never shop at a non-organic supermarket, and mammoth **Bio** (organic) shops like LPG or Bio Company are a testament to this. Outdoor markets can be found somewhere in the city every day of the week, often populated by local farmers. *Restaurants*, too, have gotten infinitely better, with many new establishments opening every year under international owners or German chefs who have spent quite a bit of time outside Germany. They wholeheartedly believe in the German food revival (**Neue Deutsche Küche** or "new German cuisine"), and aim for dishes that are innovative, fresh, and local, with firm roots in German culinary history. People of all ethnicities and backgrounds are immigrating to Germany and bringing their cuisines with them.

At last, Germans—and especially Berliners—are learning that street food can be more than just *Currywurst*, and ethnic food more than just *Döner*.

That being said, your first visit to a supermarket in Berlin will probably be an eye-opener—and not in a good way. Those who have lived in Berlin for even a couple of months know that the only essential ingredient in any home-cooked meal is **planning ahead**. Those who don't know that yet simply haven't lived here long enough, or haven't attempted to cook a meal and run into the problem of Berlin's perplexingly badly stocked supermarkets. True, they're not all like this, but coming from the UK where a Sainsbury's or a Marks and Spencer will have all the basics you need, no matter the day of the week, or America, where supermarkets are the size of shopping malls, the small, modest German supermarket can seem positively enigmatic. The only explanation, really, is that

^ *Fresh* Rosenkohl *(Brussels sprouts) for sale at the Kollwitzplatz market in Prenzlauer Berg* it is there to serve modest German needs. Most Germans buy comparatively little when shopping, preferring to make trips to the supermarket frequently and buy less each time. Their tiny refrigerators are all too often a testament to this. They seem to discourage real, heavy-duty cooking by sheer size, as ambitious home cooks will quickly discover.

German law dictates that all **shops close on Sundays**, but supermarkets in train stations are bizarrely exempt from this, leading to some laughable scenes of chaos and long lines that are almost post-apocalyptic, the aisles like shopping cart versions of bumper cars at the local carnival. The supermarkets at Hauptbahnhof, for example, or Ostbahnhof might end up being your only options if you've run out of a household staple and can't wait until Monday. Unfortunately for you, the entire city is also aware of the train station exemption, and has flocked directly to these supermarkets to do their Sunday shopping as well.

German grocery shopping can often seem more like contact sport than leisurely weekend activity. So how do you get in there, find what you need, and get out? More to the point, how do you even know which supermarket to visit in the first place? Having a thorough understanding of your options is a good way to start.

DISCOUNT SUPERMARKETS

These chain supermarkets are Germany's bread and butter. They are stocked with nothing special at exceedingly low prices. You'll find yourself at these places often if you're a student or just starting out—they're really the only way to eat on the cheap without subsisting entirely on junk food. Most of them keep prices so low by keeping service, selection, and store design to a minimum. **Aldi** and **Lidl**, for example, keep products in the original shipping boxes or palettes, stacking them on top of one another and letting customers take what they need. If you place a high premium on fresh salad, you probably won't want to shop here: you'll most likely find a couple of carrots, a cabbage head, and some tomatoes. What's more, if you've forgotten just one thing and hope to make a quick run for it, don't count on just popping in. Even if you find what you're looking for instantly, you'll end up waiting in a line that snakes halfway around the shop as there's usually only one cashier working at a time. In spite of all this, Aldi can yield some treasures on occasion, since it actually owns Trader Joe's, the popular American organic chain. Every once in a while, packages of organic dried fruits and nuts labeled with the Trader Joe's logo will show up there. Once a year, during Aldi's America and Mexico week, foods appear that have little to do with the reality of living in these countries, but are rather a sort of culinary representation of what Germans think Americans or Mexicans eat. You can sometimes find good old maple syrup at a discount, American brand peanut butter, or tacos and tortillas.

Depending on the day of the week, you'll be able to find some decent salad ingredients at **Netto**, as well as a selection of organic fruits and vegetables. They have strawberries and other fruits when in season, and meats and cheeses that aren't half bad. In fact, if you don't want to spend a fortune on meat, check Netto's refrigerators often: sometimes they have good cuts for decent prices, perfect for a Sunday roast. Their frozen cases can be a decent bet for fish in a city not known for its seafood. You will also find reasonable staples like flour and sugar, and a wide array of baking ingredients. The last aisle is almost always devoted to drinks, a good percentage of which is beer.

MID-LEVEL SUPERMARKETS

The situation starts to improve—or at least normalize—at mid-level supermarkets. You'll get your token produce aisle with an expanded selection, including organic fruits and vegetables. You may be greeted by more than one sort of salad, and chances are you'll even find some fresh herbs lying around. In addition to aisles for grains, dairy, and baking supplies, you may also find a couple of deli style counters for fresh cheeses and meats by weight. Usually there is a bread section with loaves and rolls behind little windows, by no means freshly baked in house, but still much healthier and tastier than packaged, sliced toast. As always, drinks are located in their own aisle (or several) closest to checkout. If you're coming from America, which has somewhat puritanical laws governing the sale of alcohol, you will be pleasantly surprised: here, everything is available at once, though sometimes the more expensive bottles of alcohol will be under lock and key. The drinking age (or at least the beer and wine purchasing age) in Germany is 16, and you will often see warning signs at checkout that you may be asked you for ID, but this is very unlikely to happen to anyone who looks older than a teenager.

The best mid-level supermarkets are **Ullrich**, **Kaisers**, **Reichelt**, **Rewe**, and **Edeka**, but even these can vary widely depending on which branch you visit. There are not that many Rewes in Berlin, but the ones that exist are almost uniformly good, with a superior selection of fresh produce, decent cuts of meat, and sometimes even a cheese counter or butcher hidden in the back. Rewe produces its own *Feinkost* (fine foods) brand, selling pretty decent sauces, jams, chocolates, chips, crackers, and sweets alongside a number of *Bio* goods. Rewe often seems to be the focus of promotions from various food manufacturers, which means you may get free samples of cheese, spreads, yogurts and the like if you go on the right day.

The Ullrich under the S-Bahn at Zoologischer Garten can look a bit dingy at first, but more than makes up for its appearance with an excellent selection of fruits and vegetables, including some more "exotic" varieties (well, at least in Germany) like mangos, avocadoes, pineapples, and occasionally passionfruit or lychees. It also has an outstanding selection of meat: it's still one of the most reliable supermarkets to find an organic whole chicken. The international aisle provides sauces and spices for making Asian, Indian, Mexican, or Eastern European dishes.

Edeka is a franchise and therefore hard to rate, as shops vary so widely in size and selection. The most accessible Edeka (also open on Sundays and holidays) is located at Friedrichstraße station. Although small, it packs in quite a lot of fresh produce, with one of the best selections of fresh herbs in the city, as well as a variety of vegetables and salads. One of the newest Edekas and the best by far opened recently in an *Einkaufszentrum* (shopping center) on a somewhat barren stretch of Moabit close to the Birkenstraße U9 stop. When you're used to tiny sizes and meager selections, this place is a wonder: a veritable warehouse of every food and household product your heart could desire.

HIGH-END SUPERMARKETS

If your food budget is quite high and you love to cook with the best ingredients, you will no doubt end up at one of Berlin's high-end food temples. Sitting at the top of most Berliners' lists is **KaDeWe** (Kaufhaus des Westens or Department Store of the West, a monument to conspicuous capitalist consumption that still remains one of the oldest, most prestigious and best stocked department stores). KaDeWe devotes an entire floor to its gourmet food market, and can be the only place to buy some hard-to-find international ingredients, albeit at an almost painfully inflated price. There are specialist sections featuring endless shelves of coffee and tea, a wine section that could fill its own supermarket, and shelves and shelves of beautiful marmalades, jams, and condiments in all colors. There are also counters where you can sit down and order a decadent meal—like oysters and champagne or lobster tail—or buy ready-made delicacies to enjoy at home.

KaDeWe gets most of its fish from **FrischeParadies** (fresh paradise), formerly known and still sometimes referred to as Lindenberg. This fine food paradise hides in one of Berlin's strangest non-neighborhoods (a barren industrial area between Moabit and Charlottenburg) and might be everybody's one-stop-shopping destination if it weren't so far from everything—and so expensive. Frische Paradies devotes an entire section at the back to fresh fish. A refrigerated room is stocked with bunches of fresh herbs, endless sorts of lettuces, mushrooms, tomatoes, and peppers, and even some hard-to-find Asian greens and edible flowers. There are rows of fine cheeses, specialty beers and sodas, salts and peppers from around the world, and a frozen section offering ice creams and gelatos unique to the store. If you're looking for something especially weird—like tonka beans, pink peppercorns, or black Hawaiian salt—you'll probably find it here. A section to one side of the checkout is also pretty enticing, full of expert kitchen tools, pots and pans, and utensils. The shop also sells a decent selection of fresh organic breads, which go for half price at the end of the day.

Mitte Meer, a play on *Mittelmeer*, the German word for the Mediterranean, is dedicated to Italian and Spanish fine foods, and heavy on the wines, pastas, and pastries. They also have reliable fish, as well as a separate, refrigerated room full of cured meats, cheeses including fresh ricotta, and fresh herbs and vegetables. Here you can also find those conical Moroccan cooking vessels known as tagines, as well as a number of other cooking tools.

An all-around provider to businesses—very often restaurants—who need everything in bulk, **Metro** is something of a local secret: you will need a membership card to get in. Metro's butcher, fishmonger, fresh produce, and alcohol sections, all manned by a well-informed staff, would be reason enough to come here. But it also sells kitchen tools, household appliances, clothing, cosmetics, children's toys, and electronics. Getting a membership card isn't all that hard, actually, and only requires that you be a business owner or even just a freelancer. So it's worth a trip to the sprawling store, located a few minutes' walk from Ostbahnhof, to speak to the front desk about whether you're eligible.

Two chain department stores are also quite good for grocery shopping: **Karstadt**, of which there are three in Berlin, and **Galeria Kaufhof** on Alexanderplatz. Both of these have food floors with good deli counters, an outstanding selection of fresh fruits and vegetables, and a vast array of international products.

ETHNIC, ORGANIC, AND MARKETS

Not surprisingly, **Turkish supermarkets** make up a decent percentage of Berlin's grocery businesses. These places sell a wide variety of fresh produce by weight, including fresh herbs and fresh spinach that would be a lot more expensive at Berlin's high-end shops. They almost always have *halal* butchers tucked in the back, where you can get some pretty choice cuts of meat handled by experts, including lamb, which is otherwise quite difficult to find. Next to these are often cases of olives, sun-dried tomatoes, stuffed grape leaves, and tasty spreads like hummus or roast pepper. These places often have at least a small international selection, and can be your best bet for things like peanut butter, honey, or yogurt as well as unusual products like pomegranate syrup, tahini, or rosehip jam.

Bio or organic food shops used to be fairly rare to non-existent here. Now you can find them in every district and even in practically every *Kiez*. **Bio supermarkets** can be prohibitively expensive for the average Berlin shopper, but they can also be the best places to find that specialty item you may have searched high and low for. They offer a good selection of produce—especially leafy greens like kale or chard. The LPG market mentioned earlier has branches in Prenzlauer Berg and Kreuzberg that are about twice the size of a normal Berlin supermarket and extremely well stocked. You can actually buy memberships to the LPG as you would at a food co-op, priced according to the number of adults in your household. These memberships lessen the cost of every item, but can be costly themselves, so they are really only worthwhile if you shop there weekly. Bio Company shops are also all over town, and are usually smaller than LPG markets and a bit more affordable.

Asian markets are also abundant in Berlin, sometimes bigger than normal supermarkets. Visit them for all manner of soy sauces, chili and sesame oils, rices and rice cookers, frozen wonton wrappers, miso pastes, and all those Asian vegetables and herbs that are difficult to find anywhere else, like bok choy, green papaya, lotus root, or even fresh coriander. These are the best places to stock up on dry spices in bulk, green teas, plum wines, and even some international products. Asian markets, for example, are the only places to buy the moist, sticky brown sugar that is an ingredient in so many English and American baked goods. You can also find self-rising flour and corn flour here, cream of tartar, and British baking powder.

Of course, for those who love to combine the thrill of browsing and bargaining with gorgeous, leafy squares and colorful characters, there are also plenty of **outdoor markets**, many of which seem to encapsulate that special European charm you envisioned when you moved here. Many of them occur twice: once on a Saturday and once in a smaller version on a weekday. Two of the most popular Saturday markets are on Kollwitzplatz in Prenzlauer Berg and Winterfeldtplatz in Schöneberg. In addition to tables piled high with fruits and vegetables, they also have a great many stalls selling prepared foods. Kollwitzplatz offers baked potatoes or soups and stews, Winterfeldtplatz goes the international route with Russian pelmeni dumplings and a truck selling authentic Thai specialties. Other scenic and tasty markets are on Arkonaplatz in Prenzlauer Berg and Hansaplatz in Moabit on Fridays, and Karl-August-Platz in Charlottenburg, Chamissoplatz in Kreuzberg, and Boxhagenerplatz in Friedrichshain on Saturdays.

Another city favorite is the **Maybachufer** Turkish market on the banks of the Landwehrkanal on Tuesdays and Fridays. Its location at the crossroads of Kreuzberg and Neukölln has gotten increasingly popular, especially in nice weather—a veritable destination in its own right. Turkish sellers loudly hawking their wares are now joined by trendier stalls selling stationery, jams, jewelry, or prepared food, and many shoppers pick a spot by the canal to eat and drink while listening to music from busking musicians passing by. The majority of the produce at this market is certainly not organic, but it trumps all the weekly organic markets in sheer bulk and low cost. A kilo of tomatoes can end up costing only a couple of Euros, for example. For even steeper discounts, get there at the very end of the day when sellers are trying to get rid of their unsold fruits

and vegetables. You may find entire cases of pears, melons, or avocados for only a Euro each.

Berlin's **Markthallen** or market halls are experiencing a revival these days. Originally built in the 19th century to offer neighborhood residents a clean, bright, and centralized place to shop, these lovely, old-world red brick structures quickly lost some of their allure as supermarkets began to take over. Today, only four of the fourteen originals still stand under *Denkmalschutz* or historical protection. The most beloved is **Markthalle IX** in Kreuzberg, which has been renovated in the last few years and rented out to small farmers, local chefs and food obsessives. Arminiushalle in Moabit is the underdog, but fast gaining ground as interest in Berlin's market halls grows again. One last market hall doesn't quite fit in, but is probably the best of them all: the age-old, classic **Rogacki** in north Charlottenburg. This *Delikatessen* has been around since the 1920s. It is not the slightest bit trendy, but rather is perfectly satisfied to be just what it is: a place you can imagine your grandmother happily puttering around, buying the ingredients for a chicken noodle soup or pot roast.

Bring your own bags to all supermarkets except the high-end ones. If you don't, be prepared to pay: each plastic bag, called a *Tüte* in German, may only cost 50 cents, but the charge is meant to discourage customers from taking them at all. If you're annoyed by always having to remember to bring bags, pay a visit to Rossmann, the ubiquitous drugstore: at checkout you'll find nylon bags folded up in their own nylon cases, small enough to carry around in a purse or pocket.

DINING OUT IN BERLIN

Eating out here can sometimes feel like a bit of a treasure hunt, but what you turn up is often well worth the effort. Unlike Paris, you won't find a fantastic bakery on every block. Unlike New York, there won't be restaurants the whole world is talking about opening up on a weekly basis. What you will find, once you've stayed here long enough, is a few good places you'll keep going back to until you've memorized the menu, one or two spots you'll reserve for a special occasion, and a

< *Fresh fruit for sale at Boxhagener Platz in Friedrichshain*

top-ten list that will more or less never waver. Discovering them all can be one of the best parts about slowly but surely becoming a local, and this book is not about to steal that experience away from you by presuming to know the best or merely listing the personal favorites of the author. But it will tell you what to expect when you get there.

You may hear a lot about Berlin's **general curtness** and lack of good service, how waiters are uniformly rude because they know they won't be tipped anyway, and how the entire staff seems to disappear the moment you want to pay. Everyone has a restaurant horror story that can be used to generalize, but that doesn't necessarily make any of it true. Knowing where you are and what kind of service is to be found there can go a long way towards holding your expectations in check, making sure you don't end a meal exasperated and neither does your server.

The service at **Michelin-starred restaurants** is likely to be top-notch ... and international. Since only a small percentage of actual Berliners would want to spend a fortune on a restaurant meal—and indeed, an even smaller percentage would have a fortune to spend in the first place—the most expensive places assume they'll be welcoming a clientele from around the world, and train their staff accordingly. Although the odd waiter may humor you by allowing you to practice your German, most of them will be enthusiastic about speaking English, if only to prove that they can.

At mid-level restaurants, where you can expect each person to pay 25 Euros or less, you can experience a bit of harried brusqueness mixed with indifference, unless you know the owner. It's **the low-end places**—the corner Turkish kebab shop or the cheapest *Currywurst* stand in your area—that, strangely enough, can end up being staffed by the friendliest and most interesting people. These people have been here for years or even decades doing what they do, serving the same grilled sausage on a roll to hundreds daily. The only thing that breaks up the monotony is the jokes they tell each other and the stories they tell you. They are often beloved neighborhood characters who see and hear all, could make a falafel or put toppings on a pizza in their sleep, and are interested in human interaction. Strike up a conversation and they'll give you something more valuable than food for your effort.

There are other typically German quirks you'll encounter here. Ask for *Leitungswasser* (tap water) at most restaurants, for example, and you may be met with a sneer. (Just as in France, waiters here are aware that that's an extra bit of money they're going to lose.) Ask for water in addition to a paid drink, however, and you'll probably be given a thimble-sized glassful—enough for one or two sips before it's gone. Most Germans, who may buy their water bottled and in bulk, regard the drinking of tap water as neither a privilege nor a right, but merely strange and perhaps tasteless.

If you've ever gone out to a meal in Berlin with German dining companions, you've no doubt been given a lesson in German tipping (known as *Trinkgeld* or "drink money"). There's truly no hard and fast rule about how much money to leave after a meal, but there are some guidelines to follow: If you're at a café without table service, which instead requires that you order everything up front (*Selbstbedienung* or "self service"), it is up to you whether to leave anything. They'll usually have a tip jar, and dropping in a few coins should be sufficient. If you order from a front counter but a member of the wait staff still brings your order to a table, give a little bit more. If you're at a café with sit-down service, and your order comes in at under 10 Euros, it is acceptable to leave a tip that merely rounds up to the next Euro. If your lunch cost 7.20 Euros, for example, you can round up to 8, leaving an 80 cent tip. If you're at a restaurant where the meal costs between 10 and 25 Euros, you can leave somewhere between 7 and 10% as a tip (again, Germans will probably warn that you've left too much). Only in cases of truly high-end dining must you raise this to around **10 to 15% of your bill**.

When you pay in Berlin, don't leave the money on the table. The waiter will tell you what you owe, to which you may add the tip. Instead of telling him how much you want in change, tell him how much you want to give him altogether. He will do the calculation and make change for you. If you don't want any change, you can give him the amount you wish to leave and just say, "**stimmt so**," which is taken as "keep the change." Keep in mind if you're out with a crowd, waiters are more than happy to split the bill and consider it completely normal.

FREE TIME AND ENTERTAINMENT

Rest assured that, whatever kind of distraction you seek out, Berlin has it. In fact, Berlin has all of them and more: theaters, jazz clubs, music halls, dance halls, museums, galleries, cinemas. Moving to Berlin can be like hitting the jackpot when it comes to arts and culture, and not just because of the variety: the prices too can seem extremely cheap in comparison to other major cities, since so much of the arts is government subsidized.

Many **performing arts** institutions in Berlin also seem to see it as their personal mission to win over a younger crowd. While frequenters of opera and classical music in New York seem to get older and older, leading prestigious opera houses to wonder where the money will come from once their current patrons are laid to rest, those scenes don't seem to suffer from the same effects of age in Berlin. On any given night at the Philharmonie (Philharmonic Hall) here, for example, you'll see a healthy mix of young and old, either dressed in finery for the occasion or sporting jeans and sneakers. Outsiders might not know it, but Berlin is a veritable **jazz** destination, attracting worldwide talent, very often thanks to the efforts of the UdK (Universität der Künste or University of the Arts) jazz department or a number of well-established clubs. **Rock and pop** acts play in Kreuzberg and Friedrichshain not only on weekends and at numerous festivals like the yearly **Berlin Festival** at the former Tempelhof Airport. The legendary techno scene is arguably Berlin's most significant musical contribution to the latter half of the 20th century.

The **museums** of Berlin's Museumsinsel (Museum Island) are among the first tourist sites touted in every guidebook, and represent a significant treasure trove. They will no doubt play a big part in your first weeks here, but you will also find that the state museums are places you can return to again and again, discovering something new on each visit. Aside from these, Berlin enjoys a wealth of astonishing independent museums—everything from the big and popular to the small and quirky. Berlin's every growing **gallery scene** has become world-renowned, featuring contemporary art by everyone from well-known stars like Ai Weiwei and Olafur Eliasson to the talented Berliners even most Berliners haven't heard of yet. **Movie theaters** run the gamut from the largest multiplex to the smallest art house cinema. And of course, every February when the city is at its darkest and dreariest, the **Berlinale** international film festival gives Berliners a reason to emerge from hibernation.

GETTING TICKETS

There's hardly a theater or opera house in Berlin that isn't selling tickets to performances online these days, but you're likely to get better deals in person—especially if you're a student. The Berlin Staatsoper or State Opera House, for example, offers half-price tickets to students as early as a month before each performance. Any unused tickets will also be sold off half an hour before curtain call at 13 Euros apiece. Furthermore, holders of the **ClassicCard**, a discount card for anyone under 30 (not just students) can get ahold of any remaining tickets an hour before the performance for 8 Euros (classical concerts) or 10 Euros (opera and ballet). The yearly ClassicCard can be bought for 15 Euros from the box office of any participating house (a list can be found on their website, www.classiccard.de).

Online portals like Hekticket (www.hekticket.de) and Berlin-Ticket (www.berlin-ticket.de) offer last-minute theater tickets. Showtime Konzert und Theaterkasse (concert and theater counter) in KaDeWe as well as two Karstadt stores—in Neukölln and at Rathaus Spandau—will also find you last-minute tickets for performances at many mainstream theaters and for events at many big clubs. Aside from that, you're best simply booking tickets directly with each venue, but don't worry too much about getting in early: except for the Philharmonic orchestra, which routinely sells out, especially when led by famed conductor Sir Simon Rattle, most classical concerts, ballets or plays will have tickets left over at the door.

Tickets to museums, be they permanent collections or special exhibitions, never have to be bought in advance. Rarely does a museum in Berlin hold such a blockbuster exhibition that a substantial queue even forms. Museums here, sadly, are treated mostly as the realm of the tourist and some of them—such as the Gemäldegalerie at the Kulturforum—can remain so empty they seem to echo. Tickets to Berlin's state museums (on Museum Island and the Kulturforum) cost between 8 and 12 Euros, and special area tickets can be bought for the museums on Museum Island or for those that are part of the Kulturforum. Annual membership cards are offered with various perks for 25, 50, or 100 Euros.

Even **movie tickets** can be quite reasonable in comparison to those in other major cities. Smaller, independent cinemas are always cheaper than the large, mainstream movie houses, but even they offer discounts Monday or Tuesday night. What's more, in a positively brilliant move that may leave some foreigners shaking their heads, perplexed as to why their own home countries didn't think of it yet, all the big movie theaters in town operate on a reserved-seating basis, meaning you can pick your seats in advance and no longer have to show up an hour early to fight off the popcorn-munching masses.

THEATER

Theater in Berlin is one of its most hallowed arts—subversive or classic, serious or wickedly funny, Berlin theaters have long been renowned for their ability to turn boring clichés and mainstream beliefs on their heads, questioning the establishment even when the establishment was the East German government and might have had them arrested, locked up, or worse. If you're a theater lover, you've definitely come to the right place, but you may have to learn some German before the full force of Berlin's wonderfully diverse theater options really begins to hit you:

- **Friedrichstadtpalast** is a stand-alone theater built in the mid-19th century. Its over-the-top shows are full of special effects, revealing costumes, and high-kicking chorus lines. It also offers more serious dance performances, and hosts traveling comedians, variety acts, and rock bands.
- **Admiralspalast** houses several theaters under one roof, offering a mixture of serious plays, comical revues, and traveling shows. It famously hosted the international version of the hit play "The Producers," which it advertised by hanging red, Nazi-esque banners on its façade. In the place of the fearful swastika, which is banned in Germany, was the black outline of a pretzel.

- **Theater am Schiffbauerdamm** is home to the **Berliner Ensemble**, a theater company founded by Bertolt Brecht in 1949, which operated in East Germany throughout the divided years. Today, its repertoire includes many classic German plays and musicals of the 20th century, including those by Brecht and the composer Kurt Weill, and translations of Russian classics.
- **Deutsches Theater** offers both classic and contemporary German theater on three different stages. A few plays every month also have English surtitles.
- **Maxim Gorki Theater** is tucked away next to Humboldt-University's stately Prussian buildings. This theater presented mostly Russian and Soviet dramas during the divided years, and now hosts a mixture of classics, literary stagings, and contemporary works.
- **Volksbühne** offers some of the most daring contemporary work in Europe, some of which is bizarre enough to make audience members squirm in their seats. The building houses two beloved "salons" that present a mixture of music performances and DJ sets, the Grüner (Green) and Roter (Red) Salons.
- **Sophiensäle** are a complex of performance spaces staging independent works of theater and dance.
- **HAU** (Hebbel am Ufer) has three separate houses offering experimental theater along with dance, multimedia presentations, and music.
- **F40** is the combined space of **Theater Thikwa** and the **English Theater**. Theater Thikwa unites disabled and

non-disabled actors onstage and bills itself as a social experiment. The English Theater presents mostly contemporary English language works, some by current Berlin playwrights.

- **Heimathafen Neukölln** presents works that highlight the local experience, sometimes to hilarious effect. It stages reimagined versions of old Berlin pieces as well as newer works about the city.
- **GRIPS Theater** is a beloved local institution—a space for performances aimed particularly at children and young people and arguably the first true children's theater in Germany.

- **Theater des Westens** had its roots in the subversive theater scene of the turn of the last century, acting as a breeding ground for some of the songwriters, composers, and performers who would define the interwar years, such as Marlene Dietrich, Bertolt Brecht, and Friedrich Holländer. In 2003, Stage Entertainment took over and now hosts international musicals, from *Les Misérables* to *We Will Rock You*.
- **Theater am Kurfürstendamm** is another historical gem: the turn-of-the-century art movement known as the Berlin Secession first met in its main hall, which was then an exhibition room and later a theater. Today it offers a mixture of classic comedies and films adapted for the stage.
- **Renaissance Theater** was responsible for the promotion and proliferation of many of Berlin's Weimar era stars, and today is home to both national and international comedy and drama.
- **Schaubühne am Lehniner Platz** occupies a modernist structure built by famed Berlin architect Eric Mendelsohn in the 1920s as the Kino Universum. It has hosted a string of provocative directors staging either contemporary works or wildly reimagined versions of classical works.
- **Haus der Berliner Festspiele** is the home theater of the Berliner Festspiele, a performing arts organization responsible for some of the best music, dance, literature, and theater festivals in town.

CLASSICAL, OPERA, JAZZ, AND POP

Of course, music also has its own hallowed place in Berlin, and as in any big city, the genres run the gamut from ear-splitting rock, punk, pop, and techno to refined classical productions. Unlike other big cities, however, you won't find only the elderly at classical and opera performances, and you won't find that the rowdier music shows are the exclusive province of the young. People tend to explore a range of options here, and aren't afraid to try new things.

The two biggest **classical music** venues are the Philharmonie, housing the Berliner Philharmoniker or Philharmonic Orchestra, and the Konzerthaus am Gendarmenmarkt. In looks, they could not be more different. The **Philharmonie** was designed by Hans Scharoun in the 1960s, and consists of the Großer Saal (large hall) and Kammermusiksaal (chamber music hall). Built as part of an attempt to transform the area near Potsdamer Platz into a lively cultural destination, it was only natural that the bizarrely original Philharmonie would be an eye-catcher. Evoking universally strong feelings in every visitor—of either love or hate—its pockmarked, yellow exterior makes it look like an underwater vessel the Beatles might have written a song about. Inside, though, it is something of a revelation, with an interior of endless staircases, and two performance spaces in which gabled audience seating surrounds the stage instead of simply facing it. It has some of the best acoustics in the world. Meanwhile, the grand, elegant Schinkel-designed Schauspielhaus, now **Konzerthaus am Gendarmenmarkt**, boasts four theaters on different levels hosting an extraordinary range of orchestras, chamber music, singers, and solo performers.

Berlin also has four **opera houses**:
- **Deutsche Oper**, also home to Berlin's Staatsballet or City Ballet, offers a mixture of classics and new works, and isn't afraid to push boundaries with more experimental stagings.
- **Staatsoper** is the more traditional of the two, though not by much: currently housed in the Schiller-Theater, it offers a mixture of classic opera, orchestral music, and ballet under the musical direction of Daniel Barenboim.

- **Komische Oper** is all glitter, feathers, sequins, and spandex, offering a mix of classics like Hänsel and Gretel and wacky original productions of its own.
- **Neuköllner Oper** offers a mixture of opera, musicals, and experimental theater. Its goal is to work to bring new productions to the stage yearly, instead of redoing the classics over and over again.

When it comes to jazz, Berlin is a real goldmine. There are so many **jazz clubs** in the city, both large and small, underground (literally) or in full view, it can take a while to sort through them. Each has a free weekly jam session where you can see local legends—as well as legends-in-the-making—strut their stuff and duel onstage:

- **Quasimodo** in the basement of Delphi-Filmpalast is a reliable stopover for some of the bigger jazz acts coming through town.
- **A-Trane** is like the living room of UdK's jazz department, where jazz professors who are also talented performers go to show off, and where students come after hours to learn from the masters.
- **Badenscher Hof** is a comfortable local bar that just happens to have great music, and is another favorite hangout of Berlin's musicians and jazz lovers.
- **Yorckschlösschen** has the look and feel of a saloon in the Wild West rather than a jazz club in Europe. Though you wouldn't know it from the charmingly shabby interior, it has also hosted its own endless list of local, national, and international greats.
- **b-flat** maintains both a devoted local following and lively tourist interest. Its floor-to-ceiling windows looking out onto Rosenthaler Straße have lured in many passersby over the years, converting them into jazz fans overnight.
- **Kunstfabrik Schlot** is literally underground, occupying a cellar in the looming brick Edison Höfe. It offers lessons and workshops to emerging jazz talents as well the opportunity to gain valuable experience performing live.
- **Waldo** features a lot of young and international acts whose sounds go way beyond the definition of straightforward jazz.

When it comes to **live music**, the biggest venue in town is **O2 World**, featuring a range of acts from classical pianist Lang Lang to rock legends like Sting. Although disparaged for ruining the alternative vibe in Friedrichshain, O2 is easy to get annoyed at but also easy to ignore in favor of all the other great venues in town:

- **Max-Schmeling-Halle** is a sports arena that also hosts concerts.
- **Tempodrom**, a tent-like structure near Anhalter Bahnhof, hosts world stars like Bob Dylan and major performance groups like Riverdance, as well as popular indie acts like Mogwai.

- **Columbiahalle** across from Tempelhofer Park, also known as C-Halle, hosts well-known indie bands as well as more mainstream favorites.
- **Huxleys Neue Welt**, at the corner of Hasenheide closest to Hermannplatz, is one of the newer venues in town, and also hosts a rotating cast of the well-known and popular or the indie and quirky.
- **Lido** hosts local and international acts and is famed for its monthly Balkan Beats dance party and indie disco.
- **Magnet Club** hosts a mixture of live music and DJs, with live acts usually taking the stage in the early evening and dance parties starting afterwards, at 11:30 at night.
- The **Postbahnhof**, originally built as a post office annex to the nearby Ostbahnhof train station, offers a variety of German and international acts playing at three different clubs.
- **Radialsystem V** is a real Berlin oddity: an old pumping station on the Spree transformed into a multi-purpose performance venue and the artistic home of Berlin dance company Sasha Waltz & Guests.
- **Waldbühne** ("forest stage") and **Wuhlheide** are set into the woods near Olympic Stadium and in Oberschöneweide respectively, open every summer for classical and rock music. Many Berliners see it as a yearly ritual to toast the summer by having a picnic at one of these outdoor music venues.

FREE TIME AND ENTERTAINMENT

FILM AND CINEMAS

You're never very far from a movie theater in Berlin, but make sure you know what language that long-awaited film is being screened in, since Germany is a country of dubbing or *Synchronisation*. When browsing for films, assume all of them are dubbed unless you see one of the following after the title: OmU for *Original mit Untertitel* (original with subtitles) or OF for *Originalfassung* (original version).

Two go-to multiplex cinemas that always offer mainstream English films in their original versions are **CinemaxX Potsdamer Platz** and **Cinestar Sony Center**. If you're looking for something with a bit more personality, however, never fear. Berlin has many fabulous old cinemas showing independent films and smaller releases, as well as some classics:

- **Babylon Mitte** hosts everything from classic black and white double features to silent films accompanied by a live orchestra or organ player.
- **Babylon Kreuzberg**, on Dresdener Straße just next to Kottbusser Tor offers a mixture of international films including originals with subtitles.
- **Kino International** is a gorgeous, futuristic Soviet-era building on Karl-Marx-Allee that screens only two films at a time in its plush, luxurious interior.
- **Hackesche Höfe Kino** offers a mixture of German and international films, usually with subtitles rather than dubbed.
- **Filmtheater am Friedrichshain** is a stand-alone theater in the Bötzowviertel. With its grand exterior staircase and double-height lobby, it can feel like one of the Hollywood cinemas of old.
- **Sputnik** Kino, a tiny cinema at the top of an old factory complex in Kreuzberg across from Hasenheide, is charmingly rough around the edges.
- **Kino Moviemento** on Kottbusser Damm looks like the favorite hangout of every film geek in town, with walls plastered over with posters and screening rooms about the size of a living room.
- **Lichtblick** Kino seems deliberately designed to look like it's on the verge of crumbling, but it is cozy and welcom-

ing, showing a mixture of arthouse films, indie releases, and old film noir.

- **Delphi-Filmpalast**, **Cinema Paris** and the **Astor Film Lounge** are elegant, historical gems in the west that hark back to an era when seeing a film was an occasion to dress your best.

Of course, because this is Berlin, and Berlin likes to move everything outdoors in summer, you can also choose from many *Freiluftkinos* or open-air cinemas between the months of May and September. Most open-air cinemas screen a mixture of beloved classics and new releases, with the only drawback being that almost all films are dubbed.

MUSEUMS AND MEMORIALS

If you're a traditional art lover, Berlin will more than satisfy your taste for painting and sculpture. If you'd rather do just about anything than stare at a picture on a wall, however, you'll probably still find yourself going to quite a few museums. Berlin has so many of them, for so many purposes, you're all but guaranteed to find that beautiful something to make your heart beat faster, or an object so perplexing it makes you wonder who thought to put it in a museum.

The **Staatliche Museen Berlin** are the so-called state museums, funded by the government and run by the Stiftung Preußischer Kulturbesitz or Prussian Cultural Heritage Foundation. Due to Berlin's years of division, the museums are still spread out among three different districts. Those on Museum Island are probably the most famous, including the **Alte Nationalgalerie**, the **Altes Museum**, the **Neues Museum**, the **Pergamonmuseum**, and the **Bode-Museum**. The Old National Gallery houses 18th century art, the Old Museum has classical antiquities of the Greeks, Romans, and Etruscans. The Bode-Museum houses the sculpture collection, while the Pergamonmuseum houses the famed Pergamon altar. The celebrated Neues Museum, which reopened in 2009 after sitting in ruins since WWII, is home to the **Egyptian collection**, including the famed bust of Nefertiti (*Nofretete* in German),

objects of pre- and early-history, and objects from the antiquities collection. Even if none of that strikes your fancy, go for the building, which was spectacularly reimagined by British architect David Chipperfield, keeping many of the museum's old details and elements of ruin visible.

The **Dahlem Museums**—the **Museum for Asian Art**, the **Museum of European Cultures**, and the **Ethnological Museum**—are some of Berlin's least visited state collections, and not just due to their remote location. These museums suffer from a lack of good PR and from a profound sense of uncertainty: most of them will be moved to Mitte, to be housed in the controversial recreation of the Prussian palace that used to sit on Schloß-platz just next to Alexanderplatz. It is hard to know when this will happen, though, as Berlin is notoriously bad at sticking to its building deadlines, and this insecure outlook definitely affects these museums.

The **Kulturforum** next to Potsdamer Platz was built in the early 1960s to compensate for the fact that most of Berlin's great treasures (on Museum Island) were now in the Russian zone. Although today it is hardly the bustling center of culture it was once envisioned as, the Kulturforum is a necessary stop on any tour of the city. Aside from the Philharmonie mentioned above, its institutions include:

^ *The Bode-Museum on Museum Island houses the sculpture and numismatic (coin) collections.*

- **Neue Nationalgalerie** designed by Mies van der Rohe is a building worth seeing on its own, a glass cube above the ground with most of its gallery space hidden underneath, dedicated to modern art.
- **Gemäldegalerie** (Paintings Gallery)
- **Kunstgewerbemuseum** (Museum of Decorative Arts)
- **Kunstbibliothek** (Art Library)
- **Kupferstichkabinett** (Copperplate Print Cabinet)
- **Musikinstrumenten-Museum** (Musical Instruments Museum)

Schloss Charlottenburg, along with its neighborhood, was named after Sophie Charlotte, wife of Friedrich I. This palace is part of a complex along the Spree surrounded by a beautiful park that also includes a pavilion and belvedere. Across the street from the Schloss in what were the palace's former stables and barracks are two more state collections and one private museum:

- **Museum Berggruen** houses modernist art by Picasso, Klee, and Matisse.
- **Museum Scharf-Gerstenberg** owns a surrealism collection.
- **Bröhan-Museum** is a private collection of Art Deco, Art Nouveau, and Functionalist objects and Berlin Secession paintings.

Aside from the state museums, the astonishing array includes:
- **Martin-Gropius-Bau**, although not a state museum, is often mistaken for one, as it is also housed in a grand 19th century building (constructed by Martin Gropius as an exhibition space in 1877). It holds temporary exhibitions of modern and contemporary art, photography, design, and architecture on its three floors, as well as a great art bookshop.
- **Hamburger Bahnhof** next to the main train station Hauptbahnhof was once a train station itself, and is now home to an extensive contemporary art collection. Its vast main hall is often used for oversized art installations of cutting-edge, international contemporary artists.
- The **Museum of Photography** next to Bahnhof Zoologischer Garten is home to the Helmut Newton Founda-

tion as well as the extensive photography collection of the Kunstbibliothek.

- The **Deutsche Kinemathek – Museum für Film und Fernsehen** (Film and Television Museum) is a good bet for those who take an interest in Germany's film industry, or just love to gawk at original movie posters, costumes, and other film memorabilia.
- The **Historiale Berlin Museum** is a great first-stop glimpse of Berlin in a nutshell. Its size and user-friendliness makes it perfect for a visit with kids—or if you crave a historical overview of the city.

- **Bauhaus Archiv** was designed by Walter Gropius, great nephew of Martin Gropius and one of the founders of the Bauhaus movement. Today, the archive is dedicated to Bauhaus art, architecture, and design.
- The **Museum der Dinge** (Museum of Things) focuses on design and everyday culture of the 20th century. It is a collection of objects and documents of the Deutsche Werkbund, a work federation of architects, artists, and builders founded in 1907.
- The **Buchstabenmuseum** (Museum of Letters) collection is a delightful jumble of letters in all colors, fonts, and sizes from all over Berlin, many of them former business signage rescued from the trash heap.
- The **DDR Museum** is a rather kitschy but fun museum that explains the history of the DDR (East Germany) through interactive displays.
- The **Computerspielemuseum** (Computer Games Museum) offers visitors the chance to play classic early computer games as well as more recent ones.

Since this is Berlin, be prepared to dive into a lot of history, all of it fascinating, much of it quite sinister:

- **Haus der Wannsee-Konferenz** was the location of the Wannsee Conference, a meeting of top Nazi officials to answer the "Jewish question."
- The **Max Liebermann Villa** was once home to the German Jewish painter and now displays many of his works.
- The **Book burning memorial** at Bebelplatz consists of empty subterranean bookshelves and hints at the approx-

imately 20,000 books, that the Nazis burned here on May 10th, 1933.

- The **Jewish Museum** houses an interactive exhibition that tells the 2,000 year history of Judaism in Europe. The jagged, lightning bolt line the museum uses as its logo is actually the shape of Daniel Libeskind's new addition: a jarring memorial and meditative space meant to commemorate the Jews who died in the Holocaust.
- The **Holocaust Memorial** is also famous for its design—an entire city block of concrete slabs of different heights and depths. Don't miss the moving and educational information center located directly beneath the memorial.
- **Topography of Terror**, an exhibition located next to Martin-Gropius-Bau right behind a preserved section of the Berlin Wall, explores the motivations behind the perpetrators of the Holocaust.
- The **Blindenwerkstatt** at Rosenthaler Straße is the rediscovered workshop of broom and brush maker Otto Weidt, who employed almost exclusively Jewish, visually impaired workers. The tiny museum tells the story of the German resistance movement in a small, personal way: Weidt fought to keep his workers from deportation, in one case personally rescuing a woman from a concentration camp.
- The **East Side Gallery** along the Spree in Friedrichshain has become more of a tourist spot than a memorial, but it showcases the restored works of the artists who painted the Wall in 1990 to celebrate the beginning of a new era.
- The **Gedenkstätte Berliner Mauer** or Berlin Wall Memorial at Bernauer Straße presents a more sobering, historical look at the Wall, complete with an information center, library, and informative guided tours.
- **Gedenkstätte Hohenschönhausen** is a museum in East Berlin's notorious former jail. A new permanent exhibition just opened here, showcasing the wide reach of communist rule, of which this space was a crucial and symbolic part.
- The **Stasi Museum** in the former headquarters of the East German Secret Police is located on Normannenstraße in Lichtenberg. In its recently reopened Haus 1 was the office of *Stasi* head Erich Mielke.

LITERATURE AND BOOKSTORES

While famous writers walked Berlin's streets over the last century and wrote about what they saw, today a whole new generation of literary hopefuls is making the city home. Berlin has a bookshop for every *Kiez* as well as every subject, and there are also some excellent English bookstores in town.

One of Berlin's most anticipated events of the year is the **Internationales Literaturfestival**, a program of city-wide readings, workshops, lectures and exhibitions. Each year has a theme, and many international talents show up to discuss their work. The elegant **Literaturhaus Berlin** on Fasanenstraße is probably best known as a great place for a meal: its Viennese style café is beloved for both food and atmosphere. Its program of exhibitions, readings, and discussions can be a great introduction to the German literary scene—if you know a bit of the language. The **Literarisches Colloquium Berlin** (LCB) at a gorgeous lakeside location in Wannsee has been a place of lively literary exchange since 1963.

A selection of Berlin's bookstores:

* **Berlin Story** is the Unter den Linden bookshop of the Berlin Story Verlag, a one-stop shop for Berlinophiles with over 3,000 titles.
* **Dussmann** on Friedrichstraße bills itself as the KulturKaufhaus (department store of culture). Taking up an entire city block, this mecca for book-, film-, and music- lovers offers everything from classics to new works, travel to cookbooks, a kids' section, an art book section, a stationery store, lots of CDs, LPs and DVDs, and even a charming separate English bookstore.
* **Buchhandlung Walter König** is an art bookstore and publisher that has several locations in Berlin, some of them in museums like Martin-Gropius-Bau and Hamburger Bahnhof, and one overlooking Museum Island.
* **Bücherbogen** under the S-Bahn at Savignyplatz offers a mixture of colorful art books for the lay art lover and academic texts on art and architecture.
* **Do You Read Me?** sells art and architecture books, highbrow magazines and periodicals in a number of languag-

es in its shop on Auguststraße and its reading room on Potsdamer Straße.

- **Pro qm** in Mitte concentrates not only on art and culture but also on politics and urban development—a worthy bookstore for a rapidly changing city.
- **Motto**, tucked into a courtyard off Kreuzberg's Skalitzer Straße, is one branch of a distribution company. Aside from the expected range of art books and magazines, Motto also sells works from small, independent publishers in limited print runs, and local literary journals.
- Travel bookstore **Chatwins** (named after travel writer Bruce Chatwin, of course) in Schöneberg sells a mixture of travel literature, guidebooks, and photography books guaranteed to give you itchy feet.
- The legendary **Marga Schoeller Bücherstube** near Savignyplatz, which has been around for nearly a century, has a nice mixture of classic and new English titles. The bookshop gained its dissident reputation for refusing to sell pro-Nazi literature in the pre-war years, and was the center of the West Berlin literary scene in the divided years.
- **St. George** sells a mixture of new and used English books in Prenzlauer Berg (Wörtherstraße).
- **Shakespeare & Sons** is the Berlin branch of the famed Prague bookstore at Raumerstraße.
- **Another Country** in Kreuzberg offers stacks of used books to burrow through, and a buyback program refunding you for books you read and then return.
- **Dialogue Books**, with former locations in both Prenzlauer Berg and Kreuzberg, has now gone fully online. It offers a lovingly curated selection of English books and also hosts great literary events.

SPORTS AND FITNESS

You may have noticed that there was already a whole section about **biking** in Chapter 6. Indeed, most Berliners see biking more as a mode of transportation (for many, the first and the best) than a mode of exercise. They wear whatever they would normally wear to work when commuting by bike (including heels or jackets and ties). Rarely will you see a Berliner in full spandex racing gear, and even then, only in particular parts of the city where racing might make sense (not on city streets, mind you). For the most part though, Germans are fitness-loving, outdoorsy types, and although it might seem like most Berliners you know would rather smoke a full pack of cigarettes and drink a few beers than go out on a jog, Berlin is actually a city full of sports appreciators, if not outright fanatics.

For instance, you'll spot many **joggers** out on the paths along the canals and the Spree, in rain, shine, or even snow. Berlin is privileged with an extraordinary amount of green space in comparison to other big cities, which means just about everyone has a favorite park or jogging route. For those who get sick of repeating the same loops, Grunewald isn't too far away, and offers enough jogging paths to satisfy and challenge any level of runner. In Prenzlauer Berg, the running track at **Friedrich-Ludwig-Jahn-Sportpark** is quite popular. In Moabit, the track at **Fritz-Schloß-Park** has exercise equipment, including balancing beams and chin-up bars.

Practically every neighborhood has its own public **Schwimmhalle** or swimming pool, some of them ornate lookers like those in Charlottenburg or Neukölln. The swimming pool at the **Velodrom** complex in Lichtenberg is probably the largest and most impressive, since it was built as part of Berlin's unsuccessful bid for the 2000 Olympics. The lakes around Berlin are more for splashing around then for serious, competitive swimming—it would be pretty difficult to swim lanes in the Tegeler See, with so many kids around. Tegeler See is quite good for boating, however, and if you're a fan of sailing especially, this lake, the second largest in Berlin, will offer you enough space to really let out your sails. Further afield there's Müggelsee in the east and the Havel and Wannsee in the west, all of which are big enough to boat, sail, or even windsurf to your heart's content.

There are lots of experiences in Berlin and untold numbers of stories, and this is but one of them. Here are some other ways to connect with the city.

HELPFUL TOURS

As one would expect from a big city like Berlin, full of history, culture, and endless mix 'n' match scenes, there's a tour here for just about everything. Some of them tend to be a lot more informative than others, however, and it can be tough to figure out which are the best for your purposes. Of course, a lot are geared towards tourists, people who are only here for a week and want to learn about one aspect of Berlin in digestible bites. But these tours do little to prepare you for the reality of living here, showing you only a well-edited or sugarcoated version of the city. A few companies, however, offer tours that work just as well for the recent transplant as they do for the curious tourist, showing even those who have lived here for years a side of the city they'd never seen before.

- **Context Travel** offers in-depth tours in a number of subjects led by not just locals, but certified experts—architects, historians, art historians, and specialists—some of whom have already completed an advanced degree in the exact subject they're giving a tour about.
- **Brewer's Berlin Tours** is one of the oldest running tour companies in Berlin, begun when headman Terry Brewer guided Allied solders through the city in the 1960s. Once the Wall fell, he was in a unique position to step in as the

number one expert on the once-divided city, and since then has built his company into one of the most reputable tour agencies while keeping a level head, a local point of view, and a love for Berlin.

- **Alternative Berlin** offers a thorough introduction to the worlds of street art and graffiti, urban culture, the local art scene, and everyone's favorite: abandoned historical buildings like factories and bunkers.
- **Slow Travel Berlin** is one of the city's most popular English-language websites, an organization that seeks to encourage both locals and travelers alike to slow down and explore the city in detail instead of just scratching the surface. As a companion to the informative website, it offers a variety of walking tours from Berlin experts.

MAGAZINES

Berlin doesn't have so many print magazines in English, but the one that everyone knows has been around since 2002: **ExBerliner**. This large format expat magazine offers features on a number of subjects that affect Berlin's international population as well as theater, film, art, and restaurant reviews.

^ *Before closed shutters: Travellers are waiting at the bus stop Karl-Liebknecht-Straße near Alexanderplatz.*

The website also has a classified section with a pretty narrow range of job options (babysitting, internships), though occasionally something good pops up. Its entertaining blogs by the magazine's editors and contributors go into depth about what it's like to live in Germany, rant about German culture, and generally try to push buttons and stir up sentiments among Germans and internationals alike.

Aside from that, two others merit mention:

- **Sand Journal** is Berlin's bi-annual English literary journal, publishing prose and poetry, both originally in English and translated into English, as well as art and photography.

- **Asymptote Berlin** is a literary translation journal that shares some of its staff with Sand.

WEBSITES AND BLOGS

Luckily, what Berlin lacks in English print publications it more than makes up for in blogs and websites, many of them run by internationals who love the city at least as much as you will, a few of them run by Germans who write in English:

- **Stil in Berlin** is a German-run lifestyle blog on fashion and street style as well as restaurants, shops, galleries, and events.
- **Überlin** was started by a British couple almost the day they moved to Berlin, and has become an extremely popular online resource for information about local music and nightlife, food, culture, and events. Their observations about what it's like to find an apartment, learn German, or live in Berlin will encourage newcomers while giving old-timers a chuckle of recognition.
- **Berlin Reified** is run by an American who holds the impressive distinction of calling Berlin home for more than a decade. At first glance simply a lovely, contemplative photo journal, this blog actually offers a wealth of information about Berlin's most beautiful parks and its most elegant restaurants, cafés, and shops from someone who knows her way around the city.

- **Foodie in Berlin** and **Berlin on a Platter** are like two sides of a coin, the former cheeky and sarcastic, the latter sincere and inquisitive. Both feature a mixture of restaurant reviews, recipes, and general observations on Berlin life. Berlin on a Platter is the Berlin section of the well-known Wednesday Chef blog. Foodie in Berlin recently moved to Barcelona and will continue her blog from there, but anyone who loves dining out should still bookmark it for the wealth of excellent and hilarious reviews to be found in its archives.
- **Slow Travel Berlin** and **Strollology** are two resources for learning about the city's architecture, history, hidden places, and interesting inhabitants. Slow Travel Berlin offers a weekly newsletter with event listings.
- **Sugarhigh** is a great resource for keeping up with local happenings, but the newsletter has gotten so popular, it is almost a given that any restaurant, event, or party it features is sure to be packed to bursting.
- **Finding Berlin** is an online journal about the city with mostly German contributors and great photography.

ENGLISH-SPEAKING AND -OWNED ESTABLISHMENTS

They're hard to resist and even harder to avoid: English-owned establishments are everywhere these days, and multiplying as more internationals move to town and open businesses. Still, even though most English-speaking expats would be loath to admit it, it's nice to enter a restaurant or bar and hear the familiar tones of your own language. Besides the ubiquitous Irish pubs that provide an English-speaking haven in just about every city on earth, there are a healthy number of expat-owned bars, restaurants, and cafés where staff is more than happy to welcome locals from both their hometown and their new town.

- **St. Gaudy Café** in Prenzlauer Berg acts as a second living room for the neighborhood. Its events are intended to encourage a merging of cultures and languages, such as weekly English-German tandem meet-ups, trivia contests, movie nights, and even art classes.

- **The Dairy** is a small café and bistro directly on Helmholtzplatz, opened by a New Zealander in 2011. It hosts frequent cooking classes and occasional events that celebrate New Zealand in some way.
- **The Melbourne Canteen** in Neukölln offers full meals, coffee and cocktails, and a friendly atmosphere that would make any Aussie feel at home.
- **Redwood Bar** opened in 2012 in a modest, bare bones setting on a quiet, residential stretch of Mitte. The Californian owner and his friendly, bilingual bartenders serve up expert cocktails and a selection of imported beers.
- **Maria Bonita**, founded by an Australian, a Mexican, and a Texan, tries its hardest to make up for the years of Tex-Mex food that have left a bad taste in Berliner's mouths. The tortillas are handmade, the spices are really spicy, and the salsa is made fresh daily.
- **The Bird** in Prenzlauer Berg (Falkplatz) and Kreuzberg (Kottbusser Damm) is an all-American burger joint full of English road signs, rock 'n' roll posters, and a boisterous atmosphere.

EXPAT GUIDANCE AND RELOCATION FIRMS

There are plenty of relocation services in Berlin, but most are geared towards the well-to-do professional who has already been hired, and is moving here to begin a new work contract. For these people, time is of the essence. While they probably want to get everything done quickly, with the fewest headaches possible, they may not realize how much they miss. If you hire someone to make your transition swift and seamless, after all, you may end up missing the fact that you've gone through a transition at all. What's more, if you've gotten this far in this book, you're probably more interested in learning for yourself than outsourcing your integration.

One company, however, extends a tempered helping hand. Founded by expats who probably understand the process and its pains much better than any German, **Expath** offers group classes in some of the basics, like finding a job or apartment or getting a visa, as well as German classes for reasonable prices.

Unlike some of the German-owned relocation firms, Expath does not sell you an expensive package deal. It's not going to act as your personal butler, as some of these companies seem to portray themselves. It's not going to keep you from learning what you need to learn to become a fully integrated member of German society by doing everything for you and labeling it "assistance". But Expath will give you a pat on the back and a nudge in the right direction—and if you're really stuck, individual coaching sessions, all for only a fraction of what the relocation services charge.

GAY BERLIN

You may have heard Berlin described as a "gay mecca" or Europe's "gay capital," and indeed the city has a well-earned reputation for being gay friendly. Even in the early 20th century, back when Christopher Isherwood moved to Berlin for its excitement and openness, the city was known as a haven for gays and lesbians, and had a thriving intellectual and night-life scene as a result of their presence. Today not much has changed, and LGBTQs of any age and origin enjoy wide acceptance here, along with a correspondingly wide range of resources.

- **Siegessäule** is Berlin's premier queer magazine, offering a mixture of political and cultural news and local listings. It also runs Kompass Siegessäule, a sort of yellow pages for local businesses that are either gay-friendly or run by members of the gay community.
- **SchwuZ** is a gay community center, short for *Schwulenzentrum*, as the word *schwul* means "gay". It just moved to Neukölln from its long-time location in Kreuzberg. In addition to weekly dance parties attracting a gay crowd, it also hosts discussions, readings, and other events to support the gay scene.
- **Schwules Museum** in Schöneberg is in many ways still considered the center of gay life in the city. It celebrates gay culture and accomplishments with exhibitions, lectures, and events.

In Berlin, you're never too far from a gay bar, but most of these places are victims of their own success: as some of the wackiest and most entertaining clubs in Berlin, they fill up with Berliners of all sexual persuasions, becoming veritable destinations for anyone looking to have a good time. The king of these, of course, is **Berghain**, though due to its worldwide reputation as a techno haven, people tend to forget that it is first and foremost a gay club (until they're rejected at the door for looking too "straight," that is). Others include:

- **Roses** on Kreuzberg's party mile Oranienstraße.
- **Silver Future** on Weserstraße in Neukölln
- **Barbie Deinhoff's** in Kreuzberg
- **Hafen** and **Connection** in Schöneberg
- **Kumpelnest 3000** in Schöneberg, for an older, more established gay scene

Crucially, Berlin also offers multilingual gay assistance and services at **Schwulenberatung** (gay counseling), which helps everyone from LGBTQ newcomers who want to know where the best neighborhoods are for them to transients and refugees who may need more serious help. **Mann-o-meter** was the first gay hotline in Germany in 1985, and offers gay counseling to this day.

Every year in June, the **Christopher Street Day** Parade wends its way from Kurfürstendamm to the Brandenburg gate in Berlin's biggest gay pride celebration.

BERLIN IN BOOKS

You didn't think this book would be the only one you'd ever need, did you? Here is a comprehensive list of books about Berlin, and some on Germany in general. Classics and new works, English translations or German originals, the books on this list can only enhance your experience of the city—and may just improve your language skills as well.

ENGLISH BOOKS

The Berlin Stories by Christopher Isherwood - The quintessential "expat in Berlin" account, this book consists of two novellas: *Mr. Norris Changes Trains* (1933) and *Goodbye to Berlin* (1939). It first introduced the world to a host of colorful characters, including the infamous Sally Bowles. Readers may be pleasantly surprised to find her quite different from the character who would eventually star in the play *I am a Camera* and the musical *Cabaret*. The lesser-known *Mr. Norris* really steals the show.

The Spy Who Came in from the Cold (1963) by John le Carré - The quintessential Cold War spy novel from a man who wrote a lot of them, this book of intrigue takes place (where else?) in Berlin in the early 1960s. At its heart a psychological thriller—and one of the best ever written—this novel tells the story of a reluctant spy on one last mission. It begins and ends at the Berlin Wall in two absolutely breathtaking—and breathless—scenes.

***Berlin Noir* (1993) and other novels by Philip Kerr** - Wickedly clever, these quick-read novels are the guilty pleasure of every Berlinophile and crime fiction fanatic. The *Berlin Noir* trilogy is set in Berlin and Vienna during the rise and fall of the Third Reich. Its main character is hard to resist: a hardened detective and compulsive womanizer who, over the course of an ever-growing number of books, works first with the Berlin Police, then as the house detective at the Adlon Hotel, and then as a private detective. The snappy, noir-ish language is endlessly amusing, while the impressions of Berlin in what was its darkest and most exciting era are unforgettable.

***Stasiland* (2003) by Anna Funder** - A must for those interested in Germany's postwar history, this journalistic account of life in the DDR has a clever frame: it is written from the point of view of the Australian author, who lived and worked in Berlin just after the Wall fell. She tasked herself with collecting the forgotten stories of some of East Germany's unsung heroes and victims: people who tried to escape over the Berlin Wall and were caught, who tried to fight injustice and were beaten down, or who simply tried to live their lives without interference from the omnipresent, omnipotent *Stasi*.

***This Must Be the Place* (2008) by Anna Winger** - An expat novel for a new age, this centers on two unlikely protagonists: an American woman who moves from New York to Berlin with her husband, but doesn't quite know what to do once she gets there. Her neighbor, a has-been German actor who made a living doing voiceover work for American films, seems equally lost. Inevitably, an unconventional friendship forms, making for a story of affection and understanding across boundaries of nationality.

***My Berlin Kitchen* (2012) by Luisa Weiss** - A memoir about re-discovering a home in Berlin, this recent book is subtitled "A Love Story, with Recipes." The half-Italian, half-American, Berlin-born author is also the blogger behind "The Wednesday Chef". It's a loving account of self-discovery, self-acceptance, and homecoming. Each chapter ends with a recipe, many of them easy examples of German cooking.

Book of Clouds (2009) **by Chloe Aridjis** - This book was published in the same year as Anna Winger's *This Must Be the Place*, and the two share some striking similarities. It is also about a brooding expat (though this time Mexican) trying to find her place in a new city. Both book and protagonist are keenly aware of the multiple layers of history under Berlin's surface, which manifest themselves in passages of dreamlike surreality and eeriness. It all leads up to a violent event that, in its own tragic way, is also a part of real life in Berlin.

The Ghosts of Berlin (1997) **by Brian Ladd** - A scholarly work by an historian who has written widely on Germany, this book takes a look at Berlin's multi-layered history through its architecture, offering a surprisingly lyrical, in-depth examination of the constantly changing city. In addition to exploring Berlin's shifting post-Wall urban landscape, including buildings, memorials, and structures still in ruin, the author offers up some intriguing theories on what Berlin has to say about German identity.

Berlin Today (2010) **by Joseph Hajdu** - A keen observation on the city as it is today, Australian native Hajdu explores Berlin's attraction to young people from around the world. Taking a look at different aspects of the city's appeal, such as its present social, economic, and cultural character, Hajdu employs the perspective of both insider and outsider to analyze what makes the city tick, and, with any luck, what will make it blossom in the future.

Germania (2010) [*Germany, oh Germany*] **by Simon Winder** - A love-hate letter to Germany and the Germans, this book is part memoir, part travelogue, and part history book, written by a clever Brit who's nursed a lifelong obsession with Germany. In no particular order, Winder embarks on short snippets of storytelling, rants and raves, and educational passages on obscure bits of history, making this book a grab bag of facts and tall tales: whatever you pull out will most likely be amusing.

GERMAN BOOKS

Most of these can be found in translation, in which case their English titles appear in brackets. Additionally, some have been noted as easier reads for enterprising non-native German speakers.

Berlin Alexanderplatz (1929) **by Alfred Döblin** - Berlin's first and ultimate epic, this 1929 novel has truly transcended its roots, its title now something of a stand-in for the lesser-known world of prewar Berlin fiction. A classic tale of Berlin's underworld during the Weimar Republic and the shady characters inhabiting it, this book finds its soul, however depressive and depraved, in ex-convict Franz Biberkopf. It has been made into two films, the second a multi-part epic by Rainer Werner Fassbinder. Also in English.

Spazieren in Berlin (1929) **by Franz Hessel** - German writer and translator Franz Hessel collaborated with Walter Benjamin to produce the first German translation of Marcel Proust's *À La Recherche du Temps Perdu*. In this book, he takes inspiration from the Parisian idea of *flânerie*—aimless wandering in a city, glorified to a level of high art—to produce a series of essays on

^ *The TV Tower peeks over the train station at Alexanderplatz.*

walking in Berlin. Prized for what it revealed about everyday life in Berlin in the 1920s, this book is a great way to learn about the city from the steady perspective of an observant but wholly unexcitable native.

Jeder stirbt für sich allein (1947) [***Every Man Dies Alone*** (US) or ***Alone in Berlin*** (UK)] **by Hans Fallada** - This is probably the best known of many works by a prolific and respected German author who was in his heyday as the country spiraled into disaster in the '30s and '40s. Remarkably, it only found international success after being translated into English and

published in America in 2009, more than 60 years after its initial release. It is now a bestseller, and has made a bit of a name for the long-dead, psychologically disturbed author. It is a fictionalized account of a true story: A couple in Nazi Germany turns their grief into action after their only son is lost at war by scattering postcards with anti-Nazi messages across the city. Soon, however, their clandestine protest gets them in trouble with the Gestapo.

Das kunstseidene Mädchen (1932) [***The Artificial Silk Girl***] **by Irmgard Keun** - Think of this as the other side of Sally Bowles: a book about another young ingénue who comes to Berlin seeking fame and fortune and keeps a diary along the way. Doris spends much of the book traipsing around the city in a fur coat she has stolen in her hometown of Cologne, but our outrageous style and trappings of luxury are only a distraction in the face of the extreme poverty and suffering she also encounters. This book offers an honest glimpse into a time that has been romanticized, glorified, and vilified.

Wir Kinder vom Bahnhof Zoo (1978) [Zoo Station: The Story of ...] **by Christiane F.** - A true story, this book arose out of a series of interviews conducted by the Berlin news magazine Stern with a teenager who grew up in the notorious Gropiusstadt housing complex. Due to a number of factors, she had become a heroin addict and prostitute by the age of fourteen. One of the starkest portrayals of teen drug use and the drug and sex trade around Zoologischer Garten, this book became a sensation and was turned into a film. This is the other side of Berlin life—one that did not involve espionage and intrigue on the edge of the Iron Curtain, but rather a desperate struggle to stay alive in a city that seemed hopeless.

Der Mauerspringer [_The Wall Jumper_] (1982) by Peter Schneider - Half novel, half journalistic account, this book tells the story of those who crossed over the border between East and West Berlin, from the early years when it was more porous to later on when the journey became far more perilous. Though we tend to imagine these courageous Wall jumpers walking through fire, dodging armed guards and tripwires, this book takes a different tack. Many of them crossed over for the most mundane reasons. Many others have been forgotten entirely as they were in fact West Berliners entering East Berlin voluntarily to visit relatives, look around, or have an adventure.

Herr Lehmann [_Berlin Blues_] (2001) by Sven Regener - An account of everyday life in Kreuzberg up to and including the fall of the Berlin Wall, this book will seem familiar to any expat. This is the story of Frank Lehmann, who finds his decadent, charmed existence thrown into turmoil as he nears the age of 30, after years of working in a Kreuzberg bar and avoiding adult responsibility. It isn't difficult to see the obvious connection between Herr Lehmann's devil-may-care attitude and the anything-goes, do-nothing spirit of the city.

Russendisko [_Russian Disco_] (2000) by Wladimir Kaminer - Written by a Russian Jewish transplant to Berlin in the 1990s, this book almost immediately became a sensation when it was published and has since been made into a movie. Kaminer has been a fixture on the Berlin literary and nightlife scenes for years, hosting his own "Russian Disco" DJ night at Berlin club Kaffee Burger. The book is a series of comical vignettes about the author's first years in the city. Easy enough to read in German, perhaps because it was written by a non-native German speaker.

Neulich in Neukölln (2009) by Uli Hannemann - A humorous account of Berlin's so-called _Problembezirk_ (problem district) turned _Trendbezirk_ (trend district), this book was written by a taxi driver who has been living in Neukölln for decades. It provides a good antidote to the breathless hype about the area. If you live in Neukölln, this is a great read for the entertaining, easy-to-digest stories of a multicultural area that has changed rapidly in the last few years.

***Ein Amerikaner in Berlin* (2009) by Ralph Martin** - This humorous account of expat life in Berlin was published in German by an American author. Ralph Martin moved to Germany to follow a love interest and ended up marrying her and having two children (his second book, about the pitfalls of Prenzlauer Berg parenthood, is aptly titled *Papanoia*). Since this was translated from English for publishing, it makes for smooth, easy, and entertaining reading. Martin's early attempts at assimilation and bewilderment over German customs will seem familiar to anyone who has just moved to Berlin.

***Das Adlon Hotel* (1955) by Hedda Adlon** - This account of the Adlon Hotel and its colourful history is written by Hedda Adlon, the granddaughter-in-law of the hotel's founder Lorenz Adlon. Going from the Adlon's charmed beginnings to its destruction at the end of WWII, the author tells tales of movie stars, opera singers, nobility, businessmen, and small-time crooks, all of whom populated the lobbies, dining halls, and rooms of this monumental hotel. Her tone is one of admiration and nostalgia, and the German is just tough enough to be a challenge—but not an impossibility—for the non-native speaker.

***Heimsuchung* [*Visitation*] (2008) by Jenny Erpenbeck** - An eloquent book whose title in English doesn't quite translate, this tells the story of a century of German history through the eyes of a single house in Brandenburg and its inhabitants. Its owners include Jews who were forced to sell it at half price in the 1930s, an architect forced to flee the DDR when he was found doing "illegal" business with the west, and a family returning from Russia at the end of the 20th century. They never meet, but rather see hints of each other in leftover objects or repairs done to the house. Reading this book in German is worth it: Erpenbeck is a master of the written word, and by the end

you'll feel the book could not possibly have the same impact in another language.

In Zeiten des abnehmenden Lichts [***In Times of Fading Light***] **(2011) by Eugen Ruge** - The son of a prominent East German historian, Eugen Ruge was born in Russia and emigrated to the DDR at the age of two with his family. Now a writer, director, and translator, Ruge based this epic largely on his own story: a tale of seventy years of Communist history told through the eyes of several generations of a family.

^ *The socialist vision of education is depicted on the façade of the Haus des Lehrers (teacher's house), Alexanderplatz.*

CONCLUSION

184 | Every once in a while, usually when I'm going about some daily activity, something entirely mundane and not at all intriguing, something I could be doing anywhere, I have an epiphany. It's as sudden as a Berlin summer storm, the kind that comes and goes so quickly, as if to remind you that it may be July, but you're still in Northern Germany:

"I live here. This is my life."

The thought may seem silly, too trivial to be called an epiphany, too inconsequential, really, even to be called a thought. But the arrival of that thought—those two short sentences echoing in my brain, in all of our brains—marks the end of one kind of Berlin life and the beginning of another. Once this stops being an experiment, once it ceases to be a prolonged vacation and simply becomes real life, that's the moment when everything in this city changes, and you along with it. Some people choose to leave at that moment, capturing that dream in a bottle like a mysterious insect to be identified later, an elixir whose power one cannot know but would rather keep safely locked away. Some people cannot bear the thought of that Berlin dream becoming a reality along with its many pitfalls, its concrete and grime and its unpleasantness. So they leave, conveniently labeling their time in Berlin a life "experience" instead of just life. Those who stay, however, who stick with the city long enough that they've seen all its dark spots, watched their love turn to hate and then back to love again, will be rewarded many times over for being able to say,

Is this biker in Rixdorf, Neukölln a waschechter *Berliner?* >

"I live here. This is my life."

Not ones for unearned praise, Berliners like to label people according to whether they were born here, how long they've been here, how deep their roots go. A **waschechter Berliner** is one whose grandparents were born here, lived their lives here, and died here. But a *waschechter* Berliner is just about as rare in the city these days as a *Waschbär* (raccoon). An **echter Berliner** is merely a Berliner whose parents were also born here, still difficult enough to find now. A Berliner is one who was merely born here, without deep roots, without adjectives.

But there's a name for you too. You are a **Wahlberliner**, a Berliner by choice, just like I am. You came here because something about this city called to you, you saw yourself in its people; you saw a house or a street or a *Kiez* that could be home. You came during a time of upheaval in your life, or during a time of boredom. Maybe you came looking for a challenge. Maybe you came expecting it to be easy. Whether it ended up being both or somewhere in the middle, you found that becoming a Berliner by choice meant you had to make many other unexpected choices as well.

The knowledge that this place, this life you chose as a Berliner by choice is one entirely of your own making can be so wonderfully liberating. But it takes time, much more time than finding an apartment, or getting a job, or learning German. Better to savor it, but better not to think of it as an experiment, an escapist fantasy, or a vacation that never ends, because the reality is so much better:

"You live here. This is your life."

Welcome home.

INDEX

INDEX

WIELAND GIEBEL
DVD: MAKING OF BERLIN
ISBN 978-3-95723-033-1
Regional code: 0 (worldwide)
Audio: 10 languages (German, English, Spanish, Italian,
French, Russian, Chinese, Danish, Turkish, Dutch)
PAL/Color/4:3, 28,5 MIN, **14,99 €**

History, curiosities and prospects. How the Hohenzollern princes created Prussia and gave Berlin
a place among the European capitals. The city's glory
in the last century, its fall and rise from the ruins. What
makes today's Berlin: its people, its architecture and
its cultural life. Superb pictures and an expert analysis
by Wieland Giebel, who has edited and published several books about Berlin.

Updated 2014!

WIELAND GIEBEL
BERLIN 1933-45, 1945-89:
NATIONAL SOCIALISM AND COLD WAR
ISBN 978-3-86368-119-7
10,5 x 19,8 cm, unfolded 84 x 59,4 cm, **3,99 €**

Searching for historical traces!

Two maps of today's Berlin visualize the years of National Socialism and the years of the Cold War with
noumerous entries and many picture. Find the Berlin
Wall, the Fuhrer Bunker, Topography of Terror, memorials, museums and many more.

An astonishing, low-priced time travel.

(German edition available.)